PRAISE FOR *LETTING THE UPSIDE IN*

"This book beautifully spans two levels of coaching. There's coaching for material success and there's coaching in service to bringing forward the deeper more fulfilling dimensions of a person's life. Lori shows us how to span both dimensions. She is truly a Soul-Centered Professional Coach."

H. RONALD HULNICK, PH.D., President
MARY R. HULNICK, PH.D., Chief Education Officer
University of Santa Monica

"Lori Cash Richards has written a powerful, poetic and passionate book that teaches us to transform adversity (and everything else that comes our way) into joyful renewal. My highest recommendation!"

STEVE CHANDLER, Author of *Time Warrior*

"Lori Cash Richards has asked us to let the upside of life into our human experience. These words of great wisdom have come from a need to heal her very own heart. If you are lucky enough to meet Lori, you know that every word of *Letting the Upside In* is written from truth and you can take these words to the bank of your most inner life and allow them to show you a way of seeing with wisdom."

STELLASUE LEE, Ph.D., Author

"*Letting the Upside In* is the story of a long journey over a short distance; from the mind to the Heart. The result—a Love affair that will last forever. I was among the privileged to witness this transformation in Lori Cash Richards. Through these words it is there for you. Thank you Lori for sharing your heart, your Loving, and the unbridled wisdom within these pages."

MICHAEL MURPHY, Retired Capitalist and former CEO

"Ready to take a swim in a crystal blue sea of love? Herein is a cornucopia of gifts for you. Each of the 33 chapters holds a unique gift to be unwrapped one by one. These gifts come in varying sizes and shapes and from numerous sources: Lori's vivid night dreams, her vast mental storehouse of lifelong memories, her discerning eye for beauty in life's both simple and grand majesty, as well as her moments of personal despair. The golden thread weaving throughout is the love flowing from Lori's tender, open heart. Her words feel like cashmere, simply and softly embracing the reader as she carries you with her on her hero's journey. Her reframes, forgiveness and repeated discovery of herself as a divine being who is perfectly okay in the face of all life circumstances are simply inspirational. Her work has the facets of a finely Russian cut diamond. What a beautiful book to give to anyone who has a heart and a desire to love."

JANE LUCIEN-SCHOLLE, Multi-media Artist,
Author and Certified Landscaper

"As a mother who has struggled at times finding the right perspective to effectively raise human beings from childhood through adulthood, Lori Cash Richards' book has been like a balm to my soul. I have found rich treasures of guidance in the honesty of her journey and her insights. I would love to sit on her couch and hear her feminine voice guide me through some of life's challenges. *Letting the Upside In* comes a close second as I can curl up with her book to find some wisdom into simplifying situations that may appear to me as unnecessarily complex."

DIANNE DAIN CALLISTER, American Mothers, President

LETTING THE
UPSIDE IN

DISCOVERING THE CODE THAT GRANTS US
ACCESS TO THE EXTRAORDINARY TREASURES
CONTAINED WITHIN OUR HEARTS

LORI CASH RICHARDS

THE WINFORD GROUP • PALOS VERDES, CA

The Winford Group
Palos Verdes, CA

©2014 Lori Cash Richards
www.loricashrichards.com

Cover: Chris Molé Design and Carrie Henkel-Brito
Interior book design: Chris Molé Design
Copy editor: Kathy Eimers
Proofreading: Jessica Cash

With heartfelt gratitude, I would like to acknowledge all the writers, poets, painters, musicians, theologians, scholars, philosophers, educators, scientists, therapists and mystics I have quoted throughout this book. I thank you for your wisdom and your willingness to share it. I have included your words, photos and paintings because they have inspired, uplifted and, in many cases, transformed me. An exhaustive search was done to determine whether previously published material included in this book required permission to reprint. If there have been any errors, I apologize, and a correction will be made in subsequent editions.

The following authors and their publishers have generously granted permission to include excerpts from the following:

Gertrude Stein in Paris. ©1985 by Kent Christensen. Reprinted with permission from the artist. www.kentchristensen.com

Principles and Practices of Spiritual Psychology. ©2012 by Drs. Ron and Mary Hulnick. Reprinted with permission from the authors. www.universityofsantamonica.edu

Words Under the Words: Selected Poems. ©1995 "*Kindness*" by Naomi Shihab Nye. Reprinted with permission from Far Corner Books, Portland, OR

A Hidden Wholeness: The Journey Toward an Undivided Life. ©2004 by Parker Palmer. Reprinted with permission from the author. www.couragerenewal.org

The House of Belonging. ©1996 by David Whyte. Reprinted with permission from Many Rivers Press, P.O. Box 868, Langley, WA 98260

Everything is Waiting for You. ©2003 by David Whyte. Reprinted with permission from Many Rivers Press, P.O. Box 868, Langley, WA 98260

ISBN: 978-0-9862392-0-5
Printed in the United States of America
10 9 8 7 6 5 4 3 2 1

To my parents

Butch and Judy Cash

and to the four best gifts they ever gave me

Jeri Cash Colton

Robin Cash Clark

David Francis Cash

Kristine Cash McBrady

"Remember the truth that once was spoken:

To love another person is to see

the face of God."

Victor Hugo, *Les Misérables*

TABLE OF CONTENTS

up·side
\ˈəp-sīd\ noun

1. A positive, favorable or advantageous aspect
2. An upward movement or trend
3. Promise, potential
4. Potential for gain in a deal, situation, or transaction

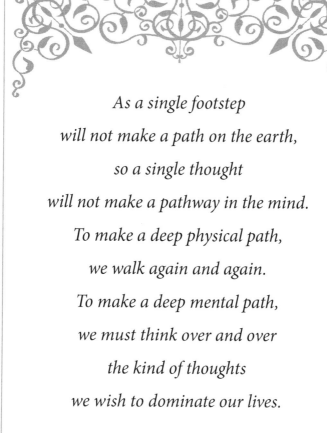

As a single footstep

will not make a path on the earth,

so a single thought

will not make a pathway in the mind.

To make a deep physical path,

we walk again and again.

To make a deep mental path,

we must think over and over

the kind of thoughts

we wish to dominate our lives.

HENRY DAVID THOREAU

LOOKING THROUGH
THE EYES OF LOVE

To see the world as it is, we must first see ourselves as we are. To see ourselves as we are, we must look through the eyes of love. When we look through the eyes of love, we see that we, like the world, are extraordinarily gorgeous creations made from, through, in and of love.

I have been trained in Spiritual Psychology to look through the lens of the spiritual consciousness. And learning to look through the lens of the spiritual consciousness changed everything. Not only did my life get better, way better—everything got more gorgeous, too. Everything.

Looking through the lens of the spiritual consciousness means cultivating a learning orientation to life while deepening in our awareness of ourselves as divine beings having a human experience. That's what changed everything.

One of the foundational principles of Spiritual Psychology as taught by Drs. Ron and Mary Hulnick, President and Chief Education Officer at the University of Santa Monica (USM), is this, "We are not human beings with souls; we are souls having a human experience. Thus, our essential nature is love."

I was first introduced to Spiritual Psychology in the fall of 2009, when I began the two-year master's degree program at USM. What made it easier for me to understand was substituting the word *loving* for the word *spiritual* everywhere I came across it. For example, to look through the lens of the spiritual consciousness is to look through the lens of the loving consciousness, in other words, to look through the eyes of love.

And, like I said, looking through the eyes of love made my life a whole lot better. So did relating to myself and others as divine loving beings. Practicing both opened up a whole new world of gorgeous possibilities.

Here's one of those possibilities: We can intentionally cultivate looking through the eyes of love, every day.

Because our essential nature is love, access to our loving is always available to us simply by attuning inwardly to it. Our loving essence is always present because it is our very nature, our natural state of being. And residing in our natural state of being means residing in wellness every day.

Isn't that just gorgeous!

And here's another possibility: Residing in wellness, identifying with and relating to ourselves as divine loving beings, makes the experience of being human better, every day.

And that's not all … Seeing through the eyes of love, infusing all we see with loving, makes us better human beings every day, too.

In fact, there's a huge upside to cultivating a consciousness of loving inside ourselves, tapping into the very essence of our being: It supports us in experientially knowing ourselves and each other as who and what we truly are—loving, creative, peaceful, joyful, beautiful and compassionate souls having a human experience.

To consciously and consistently reside in love is my ongoing intention. I live this intention perfectly imperfectly every day.

Years ago, when I was going through a tough time, a dear friend sent me a card that read, "Live imperfectly with great delight." I framed that card and hung it in my bathroom where I would see it every day.

It helps me remember this—I get to begin again, every day.

Every day is a blank slate, and I choose how to fill that slate. To fill it with love is my heartfelt intention—words of love, acts of love, gifts of love, thoughts of love, a heart full of love coming from and through a consciousness of loving.

As I attune inwardly to the essence of who and what I truly am, the following intentions support me creating an inner world of purpose, clarity, freedom, alignment and peace. They also help anchor this way of being and seeing inside of me.

- I am looking through the eyes of love, experiencing myself and others as divine beings having a human experience.
- I am awakening more fully into the awareness that we are inherently loving beings.
- I am focusing on the core of beauty, loving and wholeness that is our essence.
- I am aligning with and attuning to love.
- I am cultivating the highest of human capacities— an unconditionally loving consciousness.

What I love about Spiritual Psychology is the inclusivity, oneness and universality inherent within it. This experience of knowing ourselves as divine loving beings, as souls whose essential nature is love, is not only available to a privileged few.

It's available to all humans. Everyone. No exceptions.

As we attune to our hearts and experience each day as a blank slate waiting to be filled with love, then our lives get better, and we get better at seeing the truth of who we are.

Spiritual and political leader Mahatma Gandhi said it this way, "If you don't find God in the next person you meet, it is a waste of time looking for Him further."

We can practice finding God, looking through the eyes of love and seeing the loving essence in ourselves and in each other, at any time, on any day, and in any given set of circumstances.

I've learned through my own experience that God is compassionate and loving no matter what's happening in my life, even during those times (or perhaps especially during those times) that I feel the most imperfect. I've also learned that being made in the image of God (a divine being having a human experience) allows me to be compassionate and loving towards myself and others, too, no matter what's happening.

In fact, it's not that we are becoming more loving as we move toward this reality. We are simply becoming more aware of the loving that we already are, awakening more fully into the truth of who and what we are.

We are, at our Authentic Self or soul level of consciousness, inherently loving beings. We are, each one of us, at our core, beautiful, unconditionally loving and whole. As divine beings having a human experience, it couldn't be otherwise.

Here's how Drs. Ron and Mary Hulnick describe the first Soul-Centered Basic Skill they teach at USM:

"*Seeing the Loving Essence* is not a technique or method or anything you do. It's not really a skill at all. Rather, it has to do with how you are inside yourself while you're being with yourself or another. It's an attitude, a way of being. And this attitude, shared freely with all, is the foundation of caring relationships and the essence of all healing."

The educational process at USM is designed to bring forth the beauty, wisdom, compassion and creativity inherent in each and every human being.

Each and every human being? Really? That sounded radical to me when I first heard it. Looking back, it's like there was way too much gorgeousness being presented to let it in all at once.

So I took my time. I learned to slow down and let what I was learning settle gently around me. Eventually, what I was learning settled gently inside me, and I came into a kind of resonance with it. That's when things got a whole lot better and a whole lot more gorgeous, like I said.

I've heard it said many times at USM that the word "educate" comes from the Latin word "educare" which means "to draw out that which lies within." That's what Ron and Mary do as educators. They draw out from within their students the loving essence and soul-centered qualities that we contain within ourselves.

With that in mind, I encourage you to take your time with this book, allowing that which lies within you to be drawn out. I encourage you to let what might seem radical to settle gently around you, and eventually, within you. Then see if you come into a kind of resonance with it, like I did.

Imagine a blanket that's been crocheted with great care by the hands of someone who loves you very much being placed around your shoulders. You don't have to do anything to enjoy the warmth and comfort of this blanket that surrounds you. You simply come into a kind of resonance with it, receiving its warmth and letting it draw your own warmth out from within you.

In the same way, you don't have to do anything to enjoy the warmth and comfort of who you truly are. You simply come into a kind of resonance with it, allowing yourself to be surrounded and filled with love, then letting that love draw out from within you your own loving, the essence of who you truly are.

The idea for this book came to me in the form of a quote by American writer and poet Henry David Thoreau:

"As a single footstep will not make a path on the earth, so a single thought will not make a pathway in the mind. To make a deep physical path, we walk again and again. To make a deep mental path, we must think over and over the kind of thoughts we wish to dominate our lives."

As we cultivate our essential nature and the soul-centered qualities that get drawn out from within, we become more and more aware of the divine loving beings that we are, and it becomes infinitely easier to think the kinds of thoughts we wish to dominate our lives.

There's a beautiful kind of reciprocity at work here since

the reverse is also true. We can work from either or both directions.

As we think the kind of thoughts we wish to dominate our lives, we become more and more aware of the divine beings that we are, and it becomes infinitely easier to awaken even more fully into the awareness that our essential nature is love.

As we come into resonance with the essence of who we truly are, we begin to recognize love as our natural state of being.

Biochemist Dr. Joe Dispenza said:

"As you think certain thoughts, the brain produces chemicals that cause you to feel exactly the way you were thinking. Once you feel the way you think, you begin to think the way you feel. This continuous cycle creates a feedback loop called a 'state of being.'"

The stories in this book were designed to assist us in aligning again and again with love, creating a continuous feedback loop to the truth of who we are, connecting us to our natural state of being.

On these pages, I write about us through the lens of my own experience. I invite you to read what I've written through the lens of your own experience, to explore your own essential nature. See if the possibilities presented here resonate. See if looking through the eyes of love gives you the same leverage that it gave me. See if your life gets better and a whole lot more gorgeous.

Renowned writer C.S. Lewis said it this way:

"It is with the awe and the circumspection proper to them, that we should conduct all our dealings with one another, all friendships, all loves, all play, all politics. There are no ordinary people. You have never talked to a mere mortal ... But it is immortals whom we joke with, work with, marry, snub and exploit ... your neighbor is the holiest object presented to your senses."

This book is written from and through the Law of Spiritual Assumption. When I write from within this law, I assume that we are divine beings having a human experience, and that you, my reader, are "the holiest object presented to my senses."

In a centering process for the beginning of the day, Mary Hulnick shares the following invocation. Her words express my heartfelt prayer for each one of us.

"We ask that we may see, accept and complete whatever is brought forward in service to our deepening awareness of ourselves as divine beings having a human experience. May loving, clarity, alignment and attunement to Spirit, divine guidance and inspiration, wisdom, self-acceptance, self-compassion, self-forgiveness, gratitude and healing grace be present here and also in times ahead. And as we awaken, may we stand forward in the radiance and glory of who we are—the Unconditional Loving, Joy, Humor, Creativity, Enthusiasm, Aliveness, Vitality, Grace and Peace."

———————•—◆—•———————

May we look through the eyes of love and see ourselves (and the world) as we truly are—extraordinarily gorgeous creations made from, through, in and of love.

Lori Cash Richards
Palos Verdes, California
August 2014

As I write, destiny calls to me,

revealing the dream

that I hold in my heart,

the dream that I have

always held in my heart.

This dream, this vision,

calls me out of the world I know

and into the world of what

mythologist Joseph Campbell called

"original experience."

CHAPTER 1

WRITE WHAT'S WRITTEN WITHIN

Years ago, I had a dream.

I'm sitting on a beach looking out over the water. Into my line of sight walk five people in white robes, carrying armfuls of scrolls. They're fully alive, these five beings, animatedly talking, laughing and really enjoying themselves, happy about wherever it is they're headed.

What surprises me is this … In my dream, I'm sitting on the sand and these five people are walking on the water.

As I watch them, I hear myself saying, "Hey, I want to do that. I want to do what they're doing."

I look to my left and sitting in the sand right beside me is a steel safe with a combination lock. In a voice that is not my own, the following words come to me, "If you want to learn to do that, you're going to have to pay attention. Pay attention so I can give you the code that unlocks the safe that allows you to do what they're doing."

I wake up every day paying attention. During the night, my heart gets filled with glittering gifts; then in the morning, I unwrap each one and write what's written within.

This morning, I feel myself settling in, attuning to the gentle voice of my heart. This inner voice comforts me and offers me a sanctuary of peace and unconditional loving. Residing in this space slows me down so I can pay attention to whatever wants to be written.

As I write, destiny calls to me, revealing the dream that I hold in my heart, the dream that I have always held in my heart. This dream, this vision, calls me out of the world I know and into the world of what mythologist Joseph Campbell called "original experience."

In this new world, I can decide for myself what matters and what doesn't. I can live the dream and create the vision that my heart has so patiently held.

Dr. Mary Hulnick, my mentor, once asked me, "If there were a sacred dream that has been held in your heart from the time that you were little—a vision that you've held for yourself in this life … what would it be?"

This is it. To write what wants to be written every day. This is my sacred dream, the vision that I've held for myself in this life. My dream has led me to writing. My life, my whole life, has prepared me for this.

And my writing seems to contain the code that unlocks the safe I saw sitting in the sand. The code that's been waiting for me all these years. The code that the other voice told me about, that voice that was not my own, informing my path, my purpose, my way through this life.

It's this code that allows me to live abundantly, like those I saw walking on the water—fully alive, animatedly talking, laughing and really enjoying myself, happy about wherever it is I'm headed.

Wayne Muller, author of *Legacy of the Heart*, described abundance with such heartfelt accuracy when he wrote, "The practice of abundance is not about how much we can get; the experience of abundance arises when we feel that whatever we have is enough."

My vulnerability, my fear, will always find a gentle place within, a place of refuge and relief, a place of ongoing abundant loving. My loving is always enough. My humility, my own loving heart, will not fail me. What I have is enough. Who I am is enough.

My intention, my clear and positive intention, is to warmly express what's written in my heart, to publish peace. This is another piece of the code, the light ahead of me that illuminates the way for me to live this dream that's being born. I write and know that all is well. All is well.

I care for this new dream, for its newness and the un-expected blessings of its coming. I cannot fail. I wrap this dream in the soft blanket of my loving, cradling it in my arms, speaking softly to it with great love. I open all my senses to this experience of dreaming for myself, living my own dream while residing in the world of original experience.

Joseph Campbell described this process in which I find myself, in which we all find ourselves when we begin following our hearts and living our dreams. He called it "The Hero's Journey." He dedicated his life to discovering the hero's deed in all our stories, across many countries and many cultures.

Here's how he described those who embark on this journey:

"They moved out of the society that would have protected them and into the dark forest, into the world of fire, of original experience. Original experience has not been interpreted for you, and so you've got to work out your life for yourself. Either you can take it or you can't. You don't have to go far off the interpreted path to find yourself in very difficult situations. The courage to face the trials and to bring a whole new body of possibilities into the field of interpreted experience for other people to experience—that is the hero's deed."

Here is another piece of the code that gets revealed to me as I move into the world of original experience. This part of the code seems to have been waiting patiently for me until I worked up the courage to move out of the society that would have protected me and into that place where I get to work out my life for myself.

Here it is, that other piece of the code … The secret to living well is loving well. And the secret to loving well is centering myself in the home of my heart and trusting my dreams, the ones that were placed there before I was born, to guide me.

I hold the vision of where I am going, what this dream (that feels like both a memory and a discovery) will bring. I answer the call. I am called, called here, to the page before me, called here, to this place where my dreams have brought me.

French philosopher Pierre Teilhard de Chardin wrote:

—————— • ⬤ • ——————

"Someday, after mastering the winds, the waves, the tides and gravity, we shall harness for God the energies of love, and then, for a second time in the history of the world, man will have discovered fire."

—————— • ⬤ • ——————

We harness the energies of love as we answer the call that resides in our hearts and begin our own Hero's Journey. We move out of thinking that we need protection and into the safety and enoughness of our own loving hearts. Having discovered fire a second time, we live the secret code the journey has revealed: Living well means loving well.

Teilhard de Chardin discovered the fire of love that burns in every heart when he wrote, "You are not a human being in search of a spiritual experience. You are a spiritual being immersed in a human experience."

And as spiritual beings, we are made of love.

Every one of us. No exceptions.

Knowing that, living from and through the spiritual consciousness, is residing in the truth of who and what we are. And residing in that truth allows us to harness for God the energies of love, bringing a whole new body of possibilities into the field of interpreted experience. The radiance of our own discovery ignites the energies of love within us, expanding us.

Being made of love, we are like the ocean—limitless in our ability to expand. We expand to meet every call, every need. It's a gentle expansion, no one else may even be aware that it's happening, but we are. We are aware of the opportunity to answer the call, leave the interpreted path and set sail to explore what's on the other side.

As I set sail into these pages, the code that unlocks the safe of my heart continues to be revealed. I pay attention as I write, letting the wind, the waves, the tides, gravity and my own dreams carry me. Harnessing the energies of love, I sail into the world of original experience and write what's written within.

I look to my left and sitting in the sand right beside me is a steel safe with a combination lock. In a voice that is not my own, the following words come to me, "If you want to learn to do that, you're going to have to pay attention. Pay attention so I can give you the code that unlocks the safe that allows you to do what they're doing."

*The Endeavor brings tears to
my eyes every time I see her.
Perhaps because, while looking through
the lens of spiritual consciousness,
I see that she is an outer expression
of the inner genius of those
who created her.
She represents each one of us,
reflecting back to us the mastery of our
own engineering and the genius of the
engineer who created us.*

CHAPTER 2

WHAT IF I'M
THE ONLY ONE?

So here's something I learned that changed everything … trust what resonates. Trust what you're naturally and organically drawn to. Trust what lights you up, brings you alive, animates you.

Jalal al-Din Muhammad Rumi, the 13th century Persian mystical poet, said, "Let yourself be silently drawn by the strange pull of what you love. It will not lead you astray."

So on October 13, 2012, when I was silently drawn by the strange pull that I had to see the Endeavor before she reached the California Science Center, I trusted what resonated, got in the car and drove all over Los Angeles until I found her, the space shuttle to which I was naturally and organically drawn.

I knew she was somewhere near the airport, making her final 12 mile journey from LAX to the California Science Center, where she would be placed in a custom built hangar to rest in peace. I'd seen her gigantic tail that morning as I drove by her on the 405 freeway while she sat waiting patiently in front of Randy's Donuts.

I sit beside her today in her hangar as I write this.

I found her that night in October on Crenshaw Boulevard in Inglewood. I was one of 1.5 million people who had gathered, lining both sides of the street, to honor her proud and final journey. And now, while she rests after 19 years and 123 million miles of flight missions, I sit next to her, learning from her, celebrating her 25 trips around the earth, honoring her contribution and her service.

She brings tears to my eyes every time I see her. Perhaps because, while looking through the lens of spiritual consciousness, I see that she is an outer expression of the inner genius of those who created her. She represents each one of us, reflecting back to us the mastery of our own engineering and the genius of the engineer who created us.

We engineered her as we were engineered. We sent her into space as we were sent to Earth. She carried priceless treasures within her as we carry priceless treasures within us. She was built to serve as we were built to serve. She was created with intelligence and pure design as were we.

What I'm thinking about, as I sit beside her, is the incredible heat she experienced while traveling, while doing what she was built to do. I read that the hottest part of any space shuttle's journey is not the launch. The hottest part is the entry back into Earth's atmosphere. Returning home heats up the wings to about 3000 degrees Fahrenheit.

Through a small hole in her side, she welcomed humans into her inner space so we could explore outer space. With incredible heat outside and a steady, livable environment inside, she served as a container of the human spirit, literally. So do we, as humans. We are, each one of us, containers of the human spirit.

As women, we also contain for nine months the spirits of the children who are born through us. For 27 months cumulatively, I was the container for the spirits of my three daughters (McCall, Madison and Hadley), their space shuttle so to speak, their mothership.

It turns out that I, like the Endeavor, am able to withstand incredible heat—12 months of debilitating nausea over the course of three pregnancies (16 weeks each). As my girls entered Earth's atmosphere, like the Endeavor, I didn't fall apart. I welcomed those souls into my inner space so they could explore this earth, this outer space, on their own, as containers of their own spirits.

Fear comes up inside me sometimes, casting doubt about what I'm doing by saying things like, "Who do you think you are, writing this?! Maybe someone else could do it better."

I take a deep breath and quickly respond, "But what if there is no one else? What if I'm the only one paying this kind of attention to the Endeavor? What if I'm the only one?"

So I sit by my new neighbor now, experiencing for myself the unique blend of curiosity and freedom she generates. She sees herself only through our eyes. She has no purpose other than to carry us where we want to go, to heights to which we could not ascend without her.

Imagine the collective intelligence of all those astronauts she contained—pilots, doctors, engineers, teachers, astronomers, geologists and on and on. Like the Endeavor, we too carry incredible intelligence and wisdom within.

Her main purpose may not have been to transport people or things into space, although that's what she did for many years. Her main purpose, as I sit here beside her, seems to be to inspire us. Although she will not travel into microgravity again, she showed us what's possible, encouraging us to go everywhere, inspiring us to go beyond the borders of our perceived limitations.

The Endeavor returned to Southern California because this is where she was originally created—another lovely metaphor. She has returned home. Her main purpose lives on even after she returns home, or perhaps especially after she returns home.

One million five hundred thousand people came out of their homes, lining the streets of the route she took to her final resting place in the California Science Center. I was one of them who came to show her my deep respect and appreciation, one in a gauntlet of admirers who stood to welcome her home.

Why? Why did we line the streets?

She had flown on the back of a specially modified 747 a few days before. We came out of our homes to watch her fly above us one last time, too. Then we honored her, honored what she represented in us, by standing beside her, grounded for good, anchored to the earth's gravity now, like us. Perhaps ultimately, we lined the streets to honor her contribution and her service. She served us, taking us where we could never have gone without her.

The Endeavor never apologizes for being big, strong, resilient, powerful, designed to serve. After all her missions (300 miles above the earth), beauty remains. With durable, determined willingness, she carried her precious cargo, relating to them by taking them where they wanted to go in love, an impersonal kind of love, a very big, expansive kind of love. An unconditional love, where she didn't seem to care who got on board, where they were from or what they did for a living. She held each who entered without condition, in the safety of her masterfully assembled parts.

Her love may look the same as indifference, but it isn't. She was one with those astronauts, in their world but not of their world. Able to withstand incredible heat, she remained a safe place, a secure environment for those on board, an unconditionally nurturing spaceship pregnant with precious cargo on her voyages.

I love that the Endeavor flew on the back of a modified 747 on her final flight home to California. After completing 123 million miles worth of missions, she let someone else carry her home. There's a beautiful discipline in this, a gentle wisdom in knowing when to use her own power and knowing when to let another carry her. She allowed that 747 to serve her as she has served.

She has taught me much, this mothership who in her way loves fiercely and impersonally, holding her precious cargo for a time then letting them go in love. She brought a steady grace and a way of loving without condition to this human experience.

So following the strange pull of what I love, that October evening, did not lead me astray. I found the Endeavor sitting for the last time beneath the massive moonlit sky waiting patiently to be taken the rest of the way home. What mastery she demonstrates.

Today, three new trees are planted

where the one once stood.

These new trees are small and fragile;

however, if we look closely,

we see that through some invisible process,

they are being made big and strong

by the soil in which their roots are planted,

the same soil that nurtured

the beloved willow.

CHAPTER 3

THE SHOULDERS ON WHICH WE STAND

My friend, Lisa Bay, and her husband, Sean, named their house. They live in the center of Santa Monica on 16th Street. They were married in their garden, standing in front of the willow tree that gave their home its name: *La Maison d'Arbre* (The Tree House).

Lisa Bay loved that tree. At one of her birthday parties, we ate ice cream on the lawn then wrote messages on paper hearts and hung them from the branches. We wrote encouraging messages of love, support and hope meant to infuse the roots of the willow with life. It was dying, but we tied our hearts to it anyway, hoping we could revitalize it. We tried as best we could to convince it to remain here with us.

Lisa Bay did everything she could for that tree. She had an arborist come to take a look at it, hoping he could save it. He told her that the tree was about 30 years old, the average life span of a willow. So Lisa Bay and Sean slowly said their goodbyes to this steady friend that had witnessed them on the day they tied their hearts to each other.

A piece of the willow's trunk remains in their garden.

It continues to bless that space and the home that bears its name.

Today, three new trees are planted where the one once stood. These new trees are small and fragile; however, if we look closely, we see that through some invisible process, they are being made big and strong by the soil in which their roots are planted, the same soil that nurtured the beloved willow.

These three small trees now stand on the shoulders, so to speak, of the one that came before. Like each of us. We too stand on the shoulders of the ones who came before. And like the three little trees, we are blessed by the lives of those who grew to maturity on the same soil on which we now stand.

What I love about Lisa Bay is how she knew to save a portion of the old willow. She knew intimately of its worth and value. That piece of the willow's trunk that she saved rests behind the new trees, wordlessly encouraging them, just by its presence, to grow.

I've heard it said that for something new to be born, something old must die. It's part of the process, designed that way. I used to make those who had come before me wrong for not knowing what we know now, for not being better than they were. Now, I see that we couldn't know what we know without those who have come before. If we are, in fact, somehow better or smarter than they were, then I accept that we couldn't be nor wouldn't be without them.

It's like what English physicist and mathematician Sir Isaac Newton said, "If I have seen further, it is by standing on the shoulders of giants." So if something old must die for something new to be born, I honor that which must die, recognizing the gifts and blessings of what came before.

I rarely read the newspaper or watch the news, and when

I say rarely, what I really mean is never. But I did once, many years ago. On Sunday, August 28, 2009, I read an article by Peggy Noonan in *The Wall Street Journal* called "The Reagans and the Kennedys." I remember because I recorded what she wrote in my journal so I wouldn't forget.

Noonan quotes a portion of a speech President Reagan gave about John F. Kennedy at a fundraiser for the JFK Library at the home of Ted Kennedy in McLean, Virginia (my own home town, the very soil on which I grew up).

Here's what President Reagan said, "It always seemed to me that JFK was a man of the most interesting contradictions, very American contradictions … One sensed that he loved mankind as it was, in spite of itself, and he had little patience with those who should perfect what was not meant to be perfect."

Noonan reports that the next morning, after the speech, Ted Kennedy sent a hand written note to President Reagan. He wrote, "I only wish Jack could have been there too last night. Your presence was such a magnificent tribute to my brother … The country is well served by your eloquent graceful leadership Mr. President." He signed it, "With my prayers and thanks for you as you lead us through these difficult times."

What touches me about this exchange is the genuine kindness coming from both sides, the magnificent tribute to what's possible that these two men left, both gone now. There's a balance and gentleness inherent in their words, coming from and through both Reagan and Kennedy, a moment of peace, possibly a moment, recorded forever now in the annals of history, of eloquent, graceful perfection.

Like that piece of the willow's trunk that rests behind the new trees in Lisa Bay's garden, Reagan and Kennedy's heartfelt exchange encourages us to continue to grow, allowing what was not meant to be perfect to be deeply loved, in spite of itself. I smile with gratitude for the example they left us with their words, for the shoulders on which we now stand, for the kindness and wisdom of their souls regardless of politics.

"If I have seen further, it is by standing on the shoulders of giants."

SIR ISAAC NEWTON

*So if something old must die
for something new to be born,
I honor that which must die,
recognizing the gifts and blessings
of what came before.*

Poet David Whyte reframed

the darkness for me

by calling it "sweet,"

offering me another way

of experiencing my aloneness.

His words reminded me

that it was there, in the dark,

that I experienced

I am not alone

nor am I beyond love.

CHAPTER 4

A WARREN BUFFETT-SIZED BANK ACCOUNT

I felt so excavated, exposed, unearthed after the divorce, when my 17-year marriage ended.

I'd been raised to be a devoted wife and a nurturing mother. I'd been tirelessly taught that those two roles would be my highest, noblest earthly callings.

So when I walked away from my role as wife, my regular, ordinary, well-known world turned recklessly upside down. It felt as if I were tumbling through jet-black darkness, unanchored in time and lost in an unrecognizable bumpy, bottomless abyss. Even Einstein's natural law of gravity seemed to have failed. Even those things that I thought were sure things, infallible things, failed. Or at least I thought they did; it felt like they had.

Every morning for more than a year, my tired brown eyes would open at an unthinkable hour, 4:30am. I can still see the red, cruel numbers on my alarm clock as what I thought of as my broken, shattered life began anew each day.

In that space between blessedly forgetful sleep and harsh, rude awakening, I couldn't quite locate the inescapable truth.

But within minutes, my caldron-like brain would pour its dense despair-inducing brew into my unsuspecting, forgetful consciousness. And the concentrated, dreaded blackness would coat my heart again, early every morning. The paralyzing pain would penetrate every cell until despair was the only emotion that let me know I was still among the living.

How I begged not to be.

I pleaded to be mercifully released from the excruciating torment of my heart shattering day after day, like a carefully handblown Italian crystal water goblet intentionally dropped on a hard, cold marble floor, repeatedly.

I could see the shattered crystal shards of my broken heart floating in my chest as the darkness descended, day after dreadful day. I could see the individual pieces as they moved aimlessly, not knowing how to put themselves back together again. The shattering was too perfect.

My heart couldn't be put back together, not the same way it once was. None of the ragged edges aligned with any of the jagged others. It felt as if each piece became its own lonely planet in an endless Milky Way, all the shards making up an inner universe of utter misery and total isolation. Or so I thought.

Here's the interesting thing that I'm seeing only now, many years later. My exploded galaxy miraculously held its shape. Even after being pulverized, obliterated into tiny pieces, through all that dense despair, I could still make out the shape of my very own heart. Unlike that shattered Italian water goblet that could no longer contain anything, my heart still contained love.

I did a double take the first time I saw the gold heart-shaped donor plaques on the wall at the University of Santa Monica.

My breath caught in my chest as my heart recognized its image being reflected in the shape of those separated plaques. Little gold hearts, the size of my palm, engraved in their centers with the names of each person who had donated $5000 or more to the university, were mounted on the wall.

These golden hearts, carefully arranged in the shape of a larger heart, glittered proudly on a wall of purple radiance. I approached slowly, wanting to see myself in their reflection, wanting to touch the space between each piece.

I self-consciously turned towards the other students to see if anyone was watching. Slowly, awkwardly, my right hand reached out to touch that space between each heart, that place where these separate parts would never meet, that place where these separate parts would never be pieced perfectly together.

I wonder if each one of the crystal shards of my shattered heart is worth $5000 or more. If so, then I carry within me an enormous fortune, a Warren Buffett-sized bank account. There are millions of broken pieces in there, an entire galaxy of sparkling shards.

Perhaps some of those shards became the chapters of this book. Each one transforming into its own lovely planet in an endless Milky Way, all the shards making up an inner universe of utter mystery and total inspiration.

And perhaps those spaces between the shards are what the Persian poet Rumi called "the place where the light enters." In all that darkness, brokenness and despair, the light found its way to the cracks where it could shine through and show me that my heart still held its shape, revealing to me that my heart still contained love.

My years at the University of Santa Monica woke me up to the possibility that just because my marriage was over, my life was not. I was introduced to the wisdom of 13th century poets like Rumi, as well as to the self-compassion of 21st century poets like David Whyte.

Whyte reframed the darkness for me by calling it "sweet," offering me another way of experiencing my aloneness. His words reminded me that it was there, in the dark, that I experienced I am not alone nor am I beyond love.

Here's what he wrote about the dark and letting it find me. Here's what he wrote about "darkness and the sweet confinement of my aloneness," where I discovered for myself that "the world was made to be free in."

Sweet Darkness

When your eyes are tired
the world is tired also.
When your vision has gone
no part of the world can find you.

Time to go into the dark
where the night has eyes
to recognize its own.

There you can be sure
you are not beyond love.

The dark will be your womb
tonight.

The night will give you a horizon
further than you can see.

You must learn one thing.
The world was made to be free in.

Give up all the other worlds
except the one to which you belong.

Sometimes it takes darkness and the sweet
confinement of your aloneness
to learn

anything or anyone
that does not bring you alive

is too small for you.

DAVID WHYTE
from *The House of Belonging*
©1996 Many Rivers Press

Now, my ongoing intention

is simply to cooperate,

to cooperate with what is,

to accept my life as it is,

myself as I am,

others as they are.

I'm not talking about resignation.

I'm talking about

a grateful acknowledgment

and a gentle rejoicing.

CHAPTER 5

LIFE: A SACRED JOURNEY

I speak freely now of things I would never speak of during the years when I thought it was my job to be the community PR Director, to make sure that everyone was happily getting along with everyone else. And if they weren't, to spin tales meant to alter perceptions until peace prevailed.

But it wasn't real peace. It was more like a desperate attempt to control, to establish some level of comfort.

Now, my ongoing intention is simply to cooperate, to cooperate with what is, to accept my life as it is, myself as I am, others as they are. I'm not talking about resignation. I'm talking about a grateful acknowledgment and a gentle rejoicing.

I'm nearly fifty and several of my friends have had cancer. It intrigues me to see the transformation that cancer can bring and has brought to those who I'm thinking about this morning. I learn from them what grateful acknowledgment and gentle rejoicing really are.

Colleen lives in my neighborhood. She had breast cancer a couple of years ago. I stopped by her home recently to pick up a punch bowl. I'd called ahead to say I was coming, and in her sweet, sing-songy voice she said, "Yes. Please come by. It's noon, and I'm still in my pajamas. I'm resting today so I'm not going to change. Just stop by, I'd love to see you."

I've known Colleen for many years. We've done lots of volunteer work and attended many events together. She is always beautifully dressed and so very, very kind. I've seen her be kind even when those around her were not. When I showed up to get the punch bowl, I was delighted when she answered the door in cheetah print pajamas, adorable as ever.

As we stood chatting at her front door, I could see going up her stairway a large collection of framed photographs of her family. She invited me in to take a closer look at what she spends her time doing now. I walked halfway up her stairs to stand for a moment surrounded by all those photos. Immediately, my body started tingling. It felt as if a magical alchemy was rushing through me, a blessed moment of ecstasy in everyday life.

Colleen had put so much love into this project that I could feel that love flowing all around and through me. I was one of those lucky enough to stand in the center of this sacred space. As all those generations of her family smiled at me from inside their frames, I was flooded with love as I stood smiling back.

Colleen told me that she spends her time now doing what matters to her. She doesn't wait for anyone else to decide what matters, she does that herself. She lives peacefully in the home of her heart surrounded by what she loves.

Like a cherished well-dressed holiday guest, a beautifully decorated Christmas tree, full of glittering ornaments, sat in the corner of her family room. As I approached it, Colleen explained that she'd collected the glass ornaments over many years. Some were expensive, some not so expensive. Once they were all placed together on the tree, they were just beautiful.

Like Colleen, her home is a place of peaceful contentedness, an outer reflection of her inner beauty.

She shared with me, in a matter-of-fact way, that she doesn't know how long she has. The cancer is in her liver now, a small tumor she's treating again with chemotherapy. If she goes out one day, she knows she'll need to rest the next. She asks for and receives lots and lots of support, a graciousness many of us can appreciate while never daring to ask for or receive ourselves.

Colleen seems to understand that life is a sacred journey serving spiritual purpose. She lives in an ongoing state of surrender and peace. Real peace, the kind that loving brings.

She blesses those she loves by placing herself and them in the protecting hands of God, by cooperating with what is. That's what she does. That's what matters to her. She accepts in the most faithful way the life that she's been given, gratefully acknowledging the perfect plan by gracefully receiving the precious gifts. And gently rejoicing in the greatest of all gifts, life itself.

My feet push hard against

the steady rock,

launching me into the air.

My mind erupts again with fear,

my soul in celebration,

as my body leaves solid ground,

risking what could be.

CHAPTER 6

WHAT THE WORLD NEEDS

I only want to be part of quiet things. I want to read, write, sleep, meditate, rest. I only want to participate in that which has meaning and purpose for me. I feel myself growling threateningly if anyone encroaches on the time I spend doing what matters to me. I'm ready to start something new, a new way of being or perhaps a new acceptance of the way I am now.

"We become aware of the transformation long after it has started," Piero Ferrucci wrote in *What We May Be,* one of the most breathtakingly beautiful books I've ever had the pleasure of reading. Maybe that's what's happening, I'm becoming aware of a transformation already well in the making.

A profound shift has occurred inside me, where no one else can see. I feel it in the way I move through my day, paying attention to what pulls me towards it, interests me. I have become very clear about whom I serve and from where my well-being originates. The life I have is the life I want, and it requires resources that flow from and through my own resourcefulness.

I am a workshop facilitator as well as a writer, coach and motivational speaker. Together with Alanna Authur-Chee (another coach and writer like me), we've created Epic Win Workshops for Women.

We begin our workshops with a quote that comes from one of the greatest American preachers of the early 20th century, Howard Thurman, "Ask not what the world needs. Ask what makes you come alive … then go do it. Because what the world needs is people who have come alive."

So this is the question we ask our clients at the beginning of our workshops, "What makes you come alive?"

I watched a documentary recently about Shane McConkey, an extreme skier and B.A.S.E. jumper. The term "B.A.S.E. jumping" is an acronym that comes from the names of the fixed objects from which the jumpers jump. Bridges, Antennas, Spans and Earth (cliffs, canyons, fjords and gorges).

Shane took the most radical risks, skiing off cliffs and jumping off all those fixed objects with a parachute attached to his back. Shane was such a willing jumper that he even jumped off cliffs in Norway wearing only a "flying squirrel suit," otherwise known as a wingsuit.

At first, Shane seemed reckless and out of control to me. But as he aged and as he developed a consciousness around what he was doing, I realized that he embodied what Howard Thurman was talking about.

Shane McConkey did what made him come alive.

He died when he was 39, after skiing off a cliff in Italy. He was wearing a parachute, but the binding on one of his skis didn't release. According to those with him, he went into a spin, never pulling the cord to release the chute. In seconds, he was gone.

While I feel deep compassion for those he left behind, especially his wife and their young daughter, somehow, I don't feel sorry for Shane. Something tells me he wouldn't want anyone to feel sorry for him. He died doing what he loved. He died doing what made him come alive. He lived in, what seems to me, an extreme state of aliveness. He loved skiing off cliffs. He lived for it. Knowing the risks, he died doing it.

I don't really get Shane's desire to ski or jump off cliffs, but I do get his desire to follow what he loved, to do what made him come alive. I really get that. And Shane kept doing it. He kept following what he loved, wherever it took him. He followed, in this radical way, what seemed like fun.

And like I said, as he aged, this consciousness came in. He studied what he was going to do before doing it. He considered it, evaluated the risks, and he kept jumping. The risks were always there, no matter how much thought or planning went into it. The risks never went away.

I watched Shane live on an edge that I don't live on in the physical world. He modeled for me indefatigable courage in continuing to live on that edge right up to the end. As one of his friends said, "He saw past fear and tapped into what's really possible."

He kept jumping into the unknown, and he developed over time and through risk-taking a certain willingness to keep risking, to keep living in his aliveness. My guess is … he landed a lot more jumps than he didn't.

I wrote the following paragraph months ago, before ever hearing of Shane McConkey. It may be what he understood better than I ever will:

It doesn't matter where we jump, it only matters that we jump. The same patterns repeat themselves over and over again. This is a great blessing, not something to be concerned about. It supports the jumping off anywhere, anytime, because jumping always leads to the same place, to that radical state of aliveness.

Then, after watching the documentary about Shane, I added: Everything supports the jumping, hurling ourselves into the unknown, where we meet ourselves, instead of our fear, for the first time and then over and over again as we continue jumping, tapping into what's really possible.

Shane seemed to live this in a big, obvious way—physically and visibly; and what a radical example of aliveness he left. Even those around him (his wife, his friends, his parents) encouraged him, cheered for him, loved him as he was. As he is.

I ask myself, "What's my jumping off point, my edge? What exhilarates and excites me, even scares me?"

The longest-serving First Lady of the United States Eleanor Roosevelt said, "Do one thing every day that scares you." It's a way of breaking the fear of who I tell myself I am and instead, meeting my most courageous self, that part of me who wants to know what's really possible.

Writing this book is my jumping off point, my edge. Jumping off and onto the page every day is my radical risk. That and imagining someone might actually read what I write and be inspired by it, like I was watching Shane McConkey.

I cliff jump in Idaho just about every summer with my kids, my brother, my brothers-in-law and my nieces and nephews. My parents and my sisters drive us to the places where we jump then they watch us, waiting for us in the boats. There are 31 of us now ranging in age from three months to 72. Some of us have jumped many times, and every summer, given the ages of the kids, there's at least one who's jumping for the first time. There are often lots and lots of tears. And there is always lots and lots of cheering.

I wrote the following because I wanted to capture what it feels like to jump. My heart pounds hard, every time, and I'm never perfectly certain that I will jump. I've never regretted jumping, though. I hope the same still holds true for Shane McConkey.

Risking What Could Be

Tentatively, I approach the ragged cliff, walking slowly to the edge where the rocks end and run into the lake far beneath my feet. I peek below, into the exhilarating depths of the cold sparkling water.

Body rocking, mind reeling, heart pounding, I hear my soul calling ... Jump! Jump! Jump!

But my feet stay firmly planted, rooted to the rock.

High above the water float the voices of my courageous children who have already jumped, "You can do it, Mom!" With their encouraging eyes on me, their cheers like soldiers surround me.

I feel my own eyes on me, observing patiently, watching closely, wondering ... Will I jump? Will I risk launching myself off the cliff, leaving solid ground?

My taskmaster mind takes over, insisting logic is the way through this. Yes. Logic. There's absolutely no good reason to jump and no good reason not to jump. I can jump if I want.

Will I, this time? Is it time?

I hold the sacred secrets of those who jump. I have jumped before. I know the body-born thrill of answering the call, quieting my protective mind, allowing my body to fly through the unsuspecting air.

This time is all there is, this moment. Will I jump, this time?

I am alone in this world, alone in this choice, alone in this risk. Blessedly alone.

Releasing its stranglehold on fear, my resistant mind finally releases its grip, sending the signal to my feet … Jump!

My feet push hard against the steady rock, launching me into the air. My mind erupts again with fear, my soul in celebration, as my body leaves solid ground, risking what could be.

———————— • ⬤ • ————————

Shane's biggest fear, according to his wife, Sherry, was working a nine to five job. I really get that. I really get how that wouldn't work for Shane because it wouldn't work for me either. Sherry said, "I would never have stopped him [from jumping], ever. It would be like caging an eagle."

I'll think of Shane jumping off all those high places when I jump onto the page now. Like him, I never know where it's going to take me or what might happen. I honor his aliveness. His free fall into life radically woke me up to what's possible.

I could judge him. Every life truly lived has much to judge in it. But instead of shaking my head and calling him crazy, I say to Shane McConkey, "Thank you for jumping over and over again, for not letting anyone stop you, especially you."

My guess is he still jumps with those Norwegians in the wingsuits. Unseen now, he's still there, every year, jumping. In the same way, those who jumped onto the page before me might be here with me, too. Unseen now, they're still here, jumping onto the page with me, just for the fun of it.

There's something undeniably beautiful about Shane McConkey. He embodied more fully than most what American poet Ralph Waldo Emerson wrote, "Do not go where the path may lead, go instead where there is no path and leave a trail."

Shane lived full of his own aliveness, with a sparkle in his eye and a radical polarity to his energy—live or die, but in either case, follow what you love, do what makes you come alive.

As it turns out, in some cultures,

butterflies are thought to be wish granters,

and as synchronicity would have it,

especially blue butterflies.

They often symbolize life, love or rebirth.

And that's not all.

The color blue in a butterfly

is also thought to symbolize joy

or a change in luck.

CHAPTER 7

BUTTERFLIES ARE
FREE TO FLY

I'm sitting in my car in a dark parking garage, cocooned really, in a lower level spot with lots of privacy.

Being cocooned here reminds me of those butterfly images that would come to me while transitioning between being married and divorced. I remember gluing a picture of a blue monarch butterfly in my notebook before going into the California Bank and Trust building to meet with three lawyers: my lawyer, my ex (also a lawyer) and his lawyer.

That butterfly, along with the Elton John lyrics I wrote underneath it, provided a sanctuary for me in a place that felt dangerous and unfamiliar. "Butterflies are free to fly. Fly away, high away. Bye. Bye." I needed those lyrics that day. Not to mix metaphors here, but I felt like a guppy in a shark tank.

I'd asked my dad to fly to California and go with me into that meeting. He said no. He said that I was fully capable of handling this all by myself. I'll tell you the truth … His confidence in me far exceeded my own.

Susan Jeffers wrote about this in her book, *Feel the Fear … and Do It Anyway,* "Every time you encounter something that forces you to handle it, your self-esteem is raised considerably. You learn to trust that you will survive, no matter what happens. And in this way your fears are diminished immeasurably."

The conference room where we met had huge floor to ceiling windows that faced north, towards Los Angeles International Airport (LAX). As I waited for the lawyers, I stood at those windows and watched a huge jetliner making its descent. Watching that airplane steadied me, grounded me and brought me into the peaceful present.

Like Lao Tzu, ancient Chinese philosopher and poet, said, "If you are depressed, you are living in the past. If you are anxious, you are living in the future. If you are at peace, you are living in the present."

I remember my soon to be ex walking in casually, as if getting divorced and meeting with me in a conference room was common, ordinary. I knew he was faking it. I remember cocking my head to the side and being slightly amused at the unconcerned way his sunglasses hung from his v-neck sweater, the laid-back khaki pants he wore and the indifferent swing of his leather briefcase in his left hand. I think he was even chewing gum.

Everything had changed, yet to look at him, nothing was different. The practiced casualness that amused me at the time actually makes me a bit sad now. I wonder how much he was hiding behind that carefully constructed nonchalance. There's no anger attached to it anymore. I feel a softening at the memory. He may have been trying so hard to mask so much. I was.

Lao Tzu, also the reputed author of the *Tao te Ching* and the founder of philosophical Taoism, said, "New beginnings are often disguised as painful endings." I couldn't see it at the time, but I see it now. That meeting with the lawyers, on the 11th floor of the California Bank and Trust building, was a new beginning for me. That's when I began to recognize Spirit's guidance in every moment.

I'd asked for lots and lots of guidance before I even walked into that building. The words that came to me I've repeated many, many times to my daughters when they're faced with something they don't think they can handle.

Smile and breathe. That's it. *Just smile and breathe.* Those were the words that came to me the night before, the guidance that carried me through what I thought I couldn't handle.

As I smiled and breathed and waited, the lawyers, all three of them, had plenty to say, plenty of papers to pass around, plenty of expertise. I didn't. I was a mom, dressed in a business suit, in a building that felt dangerous and unfamiliar, a stranger in a totally foreign place.

But I waited and when the time came, instead of responding in anger as I had the past, I simply smiled and said the other words that had also come to me the night before, "I have nothing further to add. I'm happy with the way my lawyer has represented me."

I wonder why those words felt like such a coup. I guess because I made a different choice. Instead of staying in blame and upset, I followed Spirit's lead. I don't know why it was so important to say those words. Maybe just for the memory of seeing my ex's jaw drop and the weighty silence that filled the room just after.

"Butterflies are free to fly." I flew away from him that day. I stopped trying to convince him and myself that I was as smart as he was, and instead, I did what felt right to me. I flew away, high away. Bye. Bye. I set myself free.

In Carol Lynn Pearson's book *Consider the Butterfly*, she wrote, "The Greek word for butterfly is the same as the word for soul. The butterfly is the only creature that changes its DNA in the process of transformation; the one that flies from the chrysalis is not the same being as the one that entered."

As it turns out, in some cultures, butterflies are thought to be wish granters, and as synchronicity would have it, especially blue butterflies. They often symbolize life, love or rebirth. And that's not all. The color blue in a butterfly is also thought to symbolize joy or a change in luck.

About a year after standing at the window in that conference room, I started dating a pilot. He, like that airplane I watched land as LAX, is steady and grounded. He also lives in the peaceful present. He may be the wish that blue butterfly glued to my notebook granted me, a change in luck, another new beginning.

The transformation from caterpillar to butterfly happens just once in the world of insects. In the world of humans, however, this transformation happens repeatedly throughout our lives. We try on wings of many colors, returning over and over again to our cocoons to smile and breathe then transform.

I didn't know a picture on a page could have the kind of power that the blue monarch did. I trusted the resonance I felt with that winged creature instead of worrying that my ex would roll his eyes and make fun of me for gluing that photo in my notebook.

That was the day I stopped caring so much about what he thought and started caring for myself. That was the day I learned to trust that I will survive, no matter what happens. That was the day I smiled and breathed and followed Spirit's lead. That was the day I flew from the chrysalis. The me who left the California Bank and Trust building was not the same being as the one who entered.

When the Namaste greeting is spoken,

it means, "My soul honors your soul.

I honor the place in you where the

entire universe resides.

I honor the light, love, truth,

beauty and peace within you

because it is also within me.

In sharing these things,

we are united,

we are the same,

we are one."

CHAPTER 8

BECOMING PART OF PEACE

Today 24 pelicans flew right over my head. Hiking 250 feet above the Pacific on the bluffs of Palos Verdes, I counted each bird as it flapped its giant wings then floated on the unseen current.

We have so many pelicans here this year. A man stopped to watch beside me, telling me that he thought it was because of all the fish populating our waters. The fish drew the pelicans here. Maybe. Or maybe the pelicans came carrying peace on their wings, placing this peace all along the western edge of our country. Perhaps they're here, these aviator emissaries, requiring nothing from us, just offering us their peace and the beauty of watching them fly.

As they soared overhead, I stood perfectly still, becoming part of their peace. Watching respectfully, I raised my hand high above my head, blocking the sun from my eyes, saluting each pelican.

Looking up at those pelicans reminds me of the year my youngest daughter, Hadley, was born in Paris. That year, we looked up at the the Eiffel Tower often because it was dotted with sparkling lights. Every half hour after dark, these lights

45

would ignite like 10,000 firecrackers, blazing for about ten minutes, then waiting for the top or bottom of the hour to begin again.

On the back side of the tower, the side facing Trocadero, was a sign that read "An 2000" which translates to "Year 2000." In 1999, the year before Hadley was born, that same sign counted down the days, one by one, until the New Year, the new century.

Hadley was born November 20, 2000. On our way home from the hospital, when she was just four days old, we stopped to take a photo of her in front of the Eiffel Tower and that sign.

The Eiffel Tower has become the icon of France. Everyone everywhere recognizes it. It was built at the turn of the last century for the World's Fair. At first it was a temporary structure and not well liked by many Parisians. There's a story about a man who, back in the early part of the last century, would take his lunch every day and sit underneath the tower just so he wouldn't have to look at it.

While I was pregnant with my Hadley, I read Ernest Hemingway's *A Moveable Feast* about his life in Paris in the 1920s with his wife, Hadley, and their young son, Bumby. Hemingway, another American expatriate and writer like me, wrote, "If you are lucky enough to have lived in Paris as a young man [or woman], then wherever you go for the rest of your life, it stays with you, for Paris is a moveable feast."

I know of two Hadleys who were lucky enough to have lived in Paris—Hadley Hemingway and Hadley Richards. Both walked the same streets and both looked up at the same Eiffel Tower.

I named my Hadley after Hemingway's wife, another American expatriate, because I wanted her to always feel a connection to her American roots, as well as to the city where she was born. I wanted my Hadley to see Paris and all of life as a moveable feast.

I have an old and precious friend named Kent Christensen. He's a painter who lives in Sundance, Utah. A painting he did of another American expatriate and writer, Gertrude Stein, comes to mind as I write about Hemingway, Hadley and Paris.

On this giant canvas that hung in Kent's New York City apartment for many years, Gertrude Stein sits comfortably on the floor of her Paris apartment with her back to the Eiffel Tower. Above her head are her words, "I like a view but I like to sit with my back to it."

What I love about Kent's painting is this: Gertrude Stein sits facing the painter so she actually becomes part of the view. She sits cross legged and round in the foreground while the Eiffel Tower sits strong and tall out through the window just over her left shoulder.

There's something so faithful to me about liking a view but sitting with my back to it. It seems to be a way of trusting that the view requires nothing from the viewer in order to exist, in order to remain. It exists, simply inviting the viewer to become part of it.

I wonder sometimes if everything in the physical world is a metaphor for something deeply spiritual. Perhaps everything we experience outside of us is meant to reflect what's inside, meant to bring whatever we can't see into our awareness.

Take peace, for example.

Our awareness of ourselves as containers of peace spans many centuries. The 21st century American writer Elizabeth Gilbert wrote about peace in her book, *Eat, Pray, Love*, "We don't realize that somewhere within us all, there does exist a supreme self who is eternally at peace."

Before her, 19th century English writer Martin Fraquhar Tupper wrote beautifully about the peace each one of us brings into the world as newborns, "A babe in the house is a wellspring of pleasure, a messenger of peace and love, a resting place for innocence on earth, a link between angels and men."

In the King James Version of the Bible (a 17th century translation of a text that spans many centuries), Christ says in John 14:27, "Peace I leave with you, my peace I give unto you: not as the world giveth, give I unto you. Let not your heart be troubled, neither let it be afraid." The New Testament, from which this text is taken, is believed to have been written during the last half of the first century AD.

Spanning the end of the 14th and the beginning of the 15th centuries, German monk Thomas à Kempis also wrote about this inner place of peace, "Let not your peace rest in the utterances of men, for whether they put a good or bad construction on your conduct does not make you other than you are."

In Hinduism, the greeting "Namaste" honors that place of peace that resides in each of us as well. It is spoken while bowing slightly, hands pressed together, palms touching and fingers pointing upwards, thumbs close to the chest. When this greeting is spoken, it means, "My soul honors your soul. I honor the place in you where the entire universe resides. I honor the light, love, truth, beauty and peace within you because it is also within me. In sharing these things, we are united, we are the same, we are one." Excavations have revealed many male and female terra-cotta figures in the Namaste posture. These archeological findings date back to 3000 BC to 2000 BC.

And returning to more recent history, spiritual teacher, author and lecturer Marianne Williamson said, "Ego says, 'Once everything falls into place, I'll feel peace.' Spirit says, 'Find your peace, and then everything will fall into place.'"

And my mentor Dr. Mary Hulnick asks the following question then answers it as part of a guided meditation, "Who am I? I am a center of pure loving awareness. And I am always at peace."

What I can tell you is that I access this place of peace within me very intentionally every day through meditation. This daily process of quieting my mind and attuning to that inner place of peace and love reminds me who I truly am—a center of pure loving awareness. And I am that, a messenger of peace and love, even when others say that I'm not or even when I don't think I am. We all are. No exceptions. This place of peace is always waiting for us, waiting for us to settle in and become part of it.

Marianne Williamson offers this prayer before attuning to that place where the entire universe resides, "Dear God, I give this time of quiet to you. Please dissolve my thoughts of stress and fear and deliver me to the inner place where all is peace and love. Amen."

What if this "supreme self who is eternally at peace, this messenger of peace and love, this center of pure loving awareness, this inner place where all is peace and love" that resides inside each of us were as easily recognizable as the Eiffel Tower? What if this place of peace became the global and universal icon of humanity and everyone everywhere recognized it in themselves and in each other?

Then we could settle in, sit comfortably with our backs to it, holding peace in our hearts and minds and trusting other human hearts and minds to do the same. Then we would know that peace requires nothing from us in order to exist, in order to remain, except for us to become part of it, like Gertrude Stein in Kent's painting.

Gertrude Stein in Paris ©1985 by Kent Christensen

What I love about Kent's painting is this: Gertrude Stein sits facing the painter so she actually becomes part of the view. She sits cross legged and round in the foreground while the Eiffel Tower sits strong and tall out through the window just over her left shoulder.

The 13th century Persian mystical poet Rumi said, "Your task is not to seek for love, but merely to seek and find all the barriers within yourself that you have built against it."

Seven centuries later, Drs. Ron and Mary Hulnick added, "Then your task is to dissolve those barriers, allowing them to return back into the nothingness from which they came."

CHAPTER 9

TRUE FORGIVENESS

Neale Donald Walsch wrote *Conversations with God*. I bought it earlier this year after hearing Neale speak in Los Angeles. I bought it because of the beautiful awareness he brought forward at the end of his speech when he invited each of us to question our assumptions and have our own conversations with God.

He's also written a children's book called *The Little Soul and the Sun*. It's a beautiful story about two young souls who enter into a sacred contract before coming to earth. One soul wants to experience what it feels like to be forgiving. The other soul, with great love, offers to hurt the little soul while on the earth so that he can experience forgiveness. The soul who's willing to serve as the one who does the hurting asks the other little soul to remember who she really is because in order to hurt him, she will have to forget her true nature. Then they celebrate by dancing across time together.

I hold this story as such a lovely possibility, not only for those two fictitious souls, for *all* souls. Neale's book opened me up to the possibility that things may not be what they seem.

They may be so much more beautiful than I have allowed myself to imagine.

Let me give you a very personal example. In 2006, I chose to leave my marriage of seventeen years. It's interesting that I continue, all these years later, to call it "my" marriage. According to a therapist we were seeing at the time, I was the "keeper of the tie."

When I finally left my post as tie keeper, rage at my soon-to-be ex-husband filled me, even though it was my choice to leave. I blamed him for everything, including never having kept a single promise he made.

This rage remained with me until I finally had the courage to admit to my mentor, Dr. Mary Hulnick, what I did not want her to know about me. I was ashamed of what I was about to tell her after graduating with not one but two master's degrees in Spiritual Psychology from the school she and her husband, Dr. Ron Hulnick, co-created over the past three decades.

"Mary," I said as I sat in her office, a sanctuary for me, "there's something I don't want you to know about me."

With her hands folded neatly in her lap, she leaned her head ever so slightly to the right, her eyes meeting mine. Gently she nodded her head, encouraging me without words to continue.

"I still feel like my ex-husband owes me. He didn't keep a single promise he made. Still doesn't. I've spent the last year with lawyers trying to collect money that is mine that he hasn't paid me. He owes me."

Mary, in her very compassionate way, nodded silently then smiling slightly, she said, "I hope you can hear what I'm about to say to you."

I'd spent the last three years paying very careful attention to every word Mary spoke. She has a way of relating to herself and others through the lens of the spiritual consciousness, through the lens of unconditional loving. I'd never experienced anything like it nor anyone who can relate with such consistency in the way Mary does. So I took a deep breath and gave her my full attention.

"While I can really appreciate how difficult it would be to have promises made to you then broken, I want to be very clear. Your ex-husband doesn't owe you anything." Then she smiled, so very gently and with such love.

"Mary," I said, my eyes wide with curiosity, "could you say more about that?"

"Of course," she replied.

Now, what she said next entered my body in such a way that I knew she was sharing with me something extraordinary and exquisitely beautiful. The tingling rush of being cleansed on a cellular level still runs through me as I write this today, a couple of years after the conversation. The divine being in Mary seemed to be communicating directly with the divine being in me, soul to soul, essence to essence. I don't have any other way of explaining it.

In fact, that's what's so magical about Mary. I've seen her relate to the divine being in everyone over and over again. She embodies the Namaste tradition: The soul within Mary recognizes, acknowledges, respects and appreciates the soul within everyone.

Here's what she said, "Lori, like I said, your ex-husband doesn't owe you anything. Although it may appear that he has broken every promise he ever made to you, he has kept at least one."

Barely able to breathe, I asked, "Which one is that, Mary?"

"The sacred contract he made with you before coming here.

The contract that has served your awakening."

"My awakening into what?"

"Your awakening into love."

Oh. I didn't get it until I got it. It came with the most unexpected sense of beauty, flooding my cells with what felt like healing energy and forgiveness.

I see now that what I was experiencing was what the writer Steve Dahl calls "true forgiveness." He writes, "If you saw the illusions for what they really are, you'd recognize you have never been slighted or harmed. You'd recognize there was never anything to forgive. True forgiveness is recognizing there is nothing to forgive."

I'd given my ex a copy of *The Little Soul and the Sun* a couple of years earlier for his birthday, but I didn't fully understand it at the time. That awareness, or even the possibility, that I had entered into a sacred contract with my ex before coming to earth and that he didn't owe me anything, that he had in fact kept his promise, totally stunned me. Then slowly, that same awareness filled me with such love, such gratitude and such compassion that I began to see the illusions for what they were. Anything I thought was missing or I thought was owed to me dissolved instantly.

The 13th century Persian mystical poet Rumi said, "Your task is not to seek for love, but merely to seek and find all the barriers within yourself that you have built against it." Seven centuries later, Drs. Ron and Mary Hulnick added, "Then your task is to dissolve those barriers, allowing them to return back into the nothingness from which they came."

Please don't misunderstand me, I still receive child and spousal support from my ex monthly as well as the arrearages that went unpaid. What I let go of was the illusion that he owed me, the assumption that I had been intentionally slighted or harmed. And letting go of that set me free.

Letting go of that set me free to dissolve the barriers I had built within myself against love; free to let love in, to live in love, from love and through love; free to imagine that one day my soul might even dance across time again with that other soul who offered to hurt me so that I could know what it felt like to be forgiving, so that I could remember our true nature and recognize there is nothing to forgive.

When we think of fear as

an acronym meant to support us,

we find that fear itself has

genius, magic and power in it.

We can use any fear that we feel

to our advantage in the moment

by remembering what FEAR really is:

Forgetting Everything is All Right.

CHAPTER 10

LET THE BIG HORSE RUN

In college, I drove a red Mazda RX7. I'm thinking about that amazing car this morning because I loved driving it. From the day I picked it up at the dealership, shiny and new, to the day I turned it in for a more practical car, I loved driving that car. It was quick, fun and the stick shift made me feel like a race car driver every time I drove it.

As a life coach, I work with people who want to get their lives in gear. Dr. Jean Houston, scholar, philosopher and researcher, said, "We all have the extraordinary coded within us waiting to be released."

That RX7 taught me how much fun releasing what was coded within could be. That extraordinary car took me everywhere I wanted to go. All I had to do was put it in gear and drive.

Many of my clients work with me to get back into the driver's seat of their lives. They're tired of feeling as if they're being driven by everyone and everything else. What they come to find out is this: Feeling tired of things as they are, sick and tired, is a very good place to be. It's a great place to be because sick and tired is what motivates them to finally get their lives in gear and drive.

So here's what we do, together … We take their lives out of neutral; we stop just revving the engine at the starting line of whatever it is they say they want; we shift into gear and we drive, pointing the car in the direction they want to go.

Let's look at an example of what it's like to be stuck in neutral, just revving the engine, going nowhere.

Imagine a race car at the starting line with other race cars along side it. Every driver has similar machinery: a car, four wheels and an engine. Before the signal that starts the race, it appears that they're racing each other. They're not.

Each and every driver is really there to see what he can do, regardless of what the other drivers can do. And knowing what he can do and where there's opportunity for improvement is good information to have. But it's information that comes only if he's willing to put his car in gear and drive.

The race starts, and all but one driver screeches out of the gate. One car remains behind, stuck. There's no problem with the car. It's in perfect working order, built to be driven. So what stopped it from participating in the race?

FEAR. Fear stopped the driver behind the wheel of that car before he even got started, fear of what he might not be capable of as well as fear of what he might be capable of. But the fear is a lie.

Why? Because we don't have any real information yet. We don't know what the driver can or can't do. Although fear seems to be the culprit, the great adversary, it isn't. Fear itself didn't stop that driver. In fact, he could have used any fear he felt to his advantage, turning it into adrenaline and blasting onto the track.

Fear itself didn't stop him, *thinking about fear* did. He let his fearful thoughts prevent what could be before it even had a chance.

Johann Wolfgang von Goethe, a German writer and politician in the late 18th and early 19th centuries, wrote, "Whatever you can do, or dream you can do, begin it. Boldness has genius, power and magic in it."

So when fear shows up, instead of letting our thoughts stop us, we can use fear as the ally it is and begin, boldly. When we think of fear as an acronym meant to support us, we find that fear itself has genius, magic and power in it. We can use any fear that we feel to our advantage in the moment by remembering what FEAR really is: Forgetting Everything is All Right.

Let me give you another example. I meditate every day. I meditate every day because slowing myself down allows really great possibilities to rise up.

During a recent meditation, a race horse rose up, presenting itself to me on the screen of my quieted mind. This horse, a thoroughbred, was young and highly spirited, born to run. I knew it had come to teach me something so I paid very careful attention.

The jockey brought it to the track as part of its training. The horse was jumpy and jittery around the other horses, prancing nervously inside the starting gate.

As I imagined that I was that race horse, one thing became very, very clear: I wanted to run. I wanted to experience the gate flying open before me and run. Run hard, all out. And what I didn't want became very, very clear as well: I didn't want anything to stop me. I didn't want to be turned out to pasture before I'd run my race. I didn't care so much about winning or losing. I cared about running, experiencing what

I was capable of. I wanted to see what I could do.

Julia Cameron in her book *The Artist Way* writes, "One trick a seasoned jockey uses is to place a green horse in the slipstream of an older, steadier and more experienced horse."

So, when I became a coach, I hired a coach. I placed myself in the slipstream of Steve Chandler, my older, steadier and more experienced coach. Then he made me laugh hard, which is sort of like running hard, because both take me right up and into my creative zone. From there, anything is possible. He also taught me to question my thoughts, especially the fearful ones that might stop me before I even get started.

I emailed that Julia Cameron quote to Steve a few months after we started working together. He sent me back a link to a song called "Let the Big Horse Run." It was originally written as a musical tribute to the Triple Crown winning thoroughbred Secretariat by singer/songwriter John Stewart. To me, it has become a reminder that boldness (letting the big horse run) has genius, power and magic in it, like Goethe said.

And Secretariat, the horse that finished 31 lengths ahead of the other horses in the Belmont Stakes in 1973, still holds the record today, over 40 years later. No horse has ever run 1.5 miles on dirt as fast as Secretariat did. He lived the life he was built for, becoming a stunning example of what it means to release the extraordinary coded within.

Whether it's race cars or thoroughbred horses, the metaphor doesn't really matter. What matters is that we see the meaning and let it inspire us, awaken that part of ourselves that wants to experience what it's like to get in gear, see what we can do, live the life we were built for.

1973 U.S. Triple Crown Winner Secretariat

*No horse has ever run 1.5 miles on dirt
as fast as Secretariat did.
He lived the life he was built for, becoming
a stunning example of what it means to release
the extraordinary coded within.*

When we slow down,

sometimes way down,

that's when we rise up and see

the beauty that is all around us,

the beauty that is always around us.

And if we slow down even more,

then we start to see

the beauty that is in us—

the preciousness, worth and value

that was there all along.

CHAPTER 11

OUR MOST PRECIOUS RESOURCE

We are our most precious resource.

Often, instead of seeing ourselves as we are, we project our preciousness, our worth and our value out into the world without seeing the projection. We make other things matter that don't really matter. We lose sight of how much we ourselves matter, of how precious, worthy and valuable we ourselves are. Instead of seeing who we already are, we look endlessly outside ourselves for what we carry inside ourselves all along.

One of the things my coach Steve Chandler taught me is to slow down because slowing down allows me to rise up. Way up. Here's what he wrote in his book *Time Warrior*:

———— ◆ ————

"Without slowing down, you get way out ahead of life itself. I'm only asking you to slow down to the speed of life. You want to dance with life, not race out ahead of life. People who race out ahead of life are falling down on the dance floor. They are living in their own futures where fear lives. But when you slow down to master this present moment, life gets fearless ... Non-linear time management stops all that weary nonsensical treading on the road to one's destiny. Rather than inching along horizontally you must simply rise up. Your life can now become vertical. Now you don't postpone challenges, you rise to them. You become a warrior. And it works."

———————— • ⬩ • ————————

So I'm a recent time warrior and a long time scuba diver. Both require slowing down to master the present moment, becoming fearless, and then rising up.

I certified as a scuba diver while studying in Israel way back in 1986. We did 13 different dives of varying depths in the Red Sea, a diver's paradise. If you're a diver, you already know, there's no way of diving fast. Scuba diving, especially deep sea diving, requires us to slow way down.

First, before every dive, we carefully check all the equipment, ensuring that we each have all the oxygen we'll need to go down and come back up. On our bodies, we carry the mask, the life vest (or BCG) and the oxygen tank with the regulator. Then we strap weights around our waists to assist us during the descent.

I remember diving way down to an eel garden on the ocean floor. There were probably eight of us certifying together. As we started down, the water around us was perfectly clear. No fish, no seaweed, no plants, nothing, just lots and lots of water.

At first, the clear water towered beneath us; then as we dove deeper, it reversed directions and towered above us. We became a school of human fish in the middle of the vast expanse of ocean.

As we swam slowly, steadily down, we couldn't talk to each other. We couldn't give the thumbs up sign either because that meant we were not okay and needed to ascend. We could only look into each other's masks, directly into each other's eyes, and that would usually tell us everything we needed to know. We would occasionally check on each other using hand signals, like the okay sign, but the deeper we went, the slower we went and the quieter we became.

Looking up and on all sides of me, I realized I was contained in a massive amount of water. It was like swimming in a huge towering building, only there were no walls or floors, just an infinite expanse of space, as far as my eyes could see, filled with water.

When we approached our destination on the ocean's floor, there were eels swaying like grass on a Willa Cather prairie as far as my eyes could see. Thousands of them. Their tails were planted in the sandy ocean floor while the current moved their long reed-like bodies. What we saw was a magic, primordial dance that goes on beneath the water even when no one is watching. As we approached the eels, they darted into the sand, completely disappearing. We were like human lawn mowers, clearing the black eel grass everywhere we went.

As slowly as we traveled down into that watery abyss, we traveled even more slowly on our way back up. There was a rope anchored to the ocean floor that had flags on it where we were meant to stop, to decompress. If we chose not to stop and ascended too quickly, we risked getting decompression sickness, otherwise known as the bends.

So we stopped at each flag, looked into each other's eyes and tried to smile, a nearly impossible act with the regulators in our mouths. Then we continued climbing up all those towering floors, acting as our own elevators, taking ourselves up to the top, back to the surface of our lives.

I don't know if what I remember is perfectly accurate. It

doesn't matter. What matters is that I remember that *I am my most precious resource.* I took myself down to those eels, slowing down, way down and mowing the eel garden, then rising back up.

In 2011, Jennie Linthorst, the founder of LifeSPEAKS Poetry Therapy, invited me to be part of her guided expressive writing and poetry therapy group. She also introduced me to her writing coach who then became my writing coach, Pulitzer Prize nominated poet Dr. Stellasue Lee.

Stellasue was the first to call me a writer, encouraging me with her own writing and her responses to what I wrote for her. "Lori, darlin', you were born to do this ... it was written into your contract for this life." And I played along, choosing to believe her.

On Tuesday nights at Jennie's, six of us gather downstairs in her lovely Manhattan Beach home for three hours. First, we read what other poets have written, poets like David Whyte, Mary Oliver, Hafiz and Dr. Stellasue Lee. Then we write our own poems, using what we've just read as a jumping off point, as inspiration.

I was 20 years old when I dove down to that eel garden. It took me another 20 years to understand that I could stop racing out ahead of life and slow down to the speed of life, like Steve Chandler said. Before I learned the value of slowing down, it took the sadness and shock of divorce to get me to slow down. And I slowed way down.

I wrote the following during a poetry therapy group on a Tuesday night at Jennie's. Other than slowing down, I'm not at all sure what I'm about to tell you has to do with scuba diving or eel gardens. This poem seems to want to be included here so I've included it, trusting it knows what it's doing.

Waking Up

My bed sits waiting for me.
My big blue bed waits for me.

I get up begrudgingly,
wishing the light would not shine
through the shutters.

I prefer darkness.
I love the darkness
when nothing is required of me.

My bed, like a steady friend, waits,
watching my coming and going,
embracing me each time I return
without asking for anything.

She receives me,
holding me in her softness,
asking for nothing in return.

While partnered with her,
I dream. I hear voices.
I see another world,
another way of being in this world.

But the real world overwhelms me.
I no longer want to claim my place in it.
Take my place. Please. Take my place.

My bed absorbs my tears, my cries,
my despair.
She holds all of it in her softness.

The world away from my bed seems
cold, dangerous, unsafe.

But not this world where I rest,
where I dream,
where my world is being reordered.

It took two years, for two years
I crawled beneath the covers.

I had no will, no way
of lifting myself out of this lesson.

So I slept,
I slept while I was waking up.

And my bed embraced me,
holding me in her softness.

I no longer let myself get so busy that I forget to slow down. I rest now. I see the beauty and practice the wisdom of underdoing it, of being quieter than ever before. As Chinese writer Lin Yutang said, "Besides the noble art of getting things done, there is a nobler art of leaving things undone."

I remember those eels, swaying slowly with the current, going with the flow, dancing way down in the silent depths of the sea. They were like cobras being seduced by the flute of an invisible snake charmer. Thousands and thousands of cobras.

When we slow down, sometimes way down, that's when we rise up and see the beauty that is all around us, the beauty that is always around us. And if we slow down even more, then we start to see the beauty that is in us—the preciousness, worth and value that was there all along. We are always surrounded by grace if we have the eyes to see it, and that grace is waiting to lift us up, as soon as we slow down.

Perhaps the depth of my despair during those two years when I dove beneath the covers of my blue bed parallels, in some elusive way, the depth of that dive to the eel garden. It was the deepest of the 13 dives we did, the scariest, the one I remember. I disappeared into my bed the same way those eels disappeared into the ocean floor. And like the ocean, love towered all around me, a massive amount of love, an infinite expanse of love, as far as my eyes could see.

When I close my eyes, I can still see those eels swaying gracefully, dancing in the wind beneath the waves. There's something about that invisible snake charmer, too. Perhaps he goes everywhere, beneath the sea to the eels and beside my bed as well. Perhaps he charmed me with his flute music while my bed held me, slowing me down so I could reconnect with my own primordial dance, so I could rise up and remember, *I am my most precious resource.*

To me, poet David Whyte's brilliance

lies in the way he shines

his 1000-watt light on every day things,

illuminating the extraordinary

in the ordinary.

His words remind me

to release the misunderstanding

or the "great mistake" of my aloneness,

coming home to myself

and joining in the conversation

happening around and through me.

CHAPTER 12

THE LIGHT SHINES ON AND THROUGH EVERYTHING

I was up late one night unpacking boxes a day or two after we moved into our California home. It was nearly midnight so the bright light shining through the sliding glass doors in the living room caught my attention. Curious, I stepped out onto the deck wondering if someone might have rented one of those big spot lights for a party.

As I stepped outside, I saw that the light was shining on and through everything. Everything was illuminated—the trees, the homes, the streets, even the street signs.

When I realized what it was, I went back into the house and woke up my husband.

"Honey," I said shaking him, "you have to come see this."

He rubbed his eyes, got up and followed me back to the living room.

"Look at that," I said, pointing to the full moon shining its corridor of white light on the ocean. "Maybe we should have paid more for this house," I whispered so not even the moon could hear me. He smiled, knowing full well we'd paid everything we had, and went back to bed.

Just down the road from us, five or ten minutes, is the Point Vicente Lighthouse. I took my daughter, Madison, and her Girl Scout troop on a tour a couple years ago. The same lighthouse keeper who has been attending to this particular lighthouse for over 35 years was our guide. He led us up the stairs to where the 1000-watt light bulb lives at the top.

I was surprised to see that the windows facing the hill, where the homes are, had been painted black. The lighthouse keeper explained that the windows had been painted so the bright light wouldn't disturb the residents who lived within its reach.

Being inside that lighthouse seemed to illuminate something inside of me. It's like I could feel that 1000-watt bulb rotating inside my chest at exact intervals. Perhaps there's black paint inside me too, a blind spot or a window where the light gets blocked so it won't disturb whatever lives within its reach.

Apparently, a ghost lives in our lighthouse. A woman who lost her lover at sea is said to have ended her life right there, her feelings of grief and aloneness driving her to jump the 250 feet off the rocky cliff and into the sea. It's rumored that she haunts the lighthouse now, still waiting for her lover's return. Perhaps that black paint gives her some privacy, too.

When I experienced my own feelings of grief and aloneness after the loss of my marriage, I certainly would have appreciated that black paint. I didn't want anyone to see the soul-shaking sadness that had me in its grip. I needed to be alone with that sadness in order to appreciate what it had come to teach me.

Here in California we have these big palm trees called Queen Palms. There are 45 of them surrounding our PV lighthouse. I counted. They're not the ones with the skinny trunks that we have everywhere in Southern California. They're sturdier.

Their trunks are thicker, more solid, and their palm leaves bigger, their canopies more beautiful.

My girls and I call them ponytail palms because when they're first planted, for about a year, their palm leaves are tied up at the top in what looks to us like ponytails. They're usually clustered together in groups of three or four, reminding us of us—girls in ponytails, clustered together in a group, relaxed and happy.

Sometimes I pass my oldest daughter, McCall, driving around town. I can hear the music blasting and see her smiling as her ponytail blows through the open window. She makes me smile that one. She came into the world kind and calm.

When she was born, I called her my Buddha baby because she rarely cried and she seemed to be fascinated by little things, like her tiny fists twirling in front of her face and the sound of her own laughter.

I still catch glimpses of all those younger versions of her when I look into her round, brown eyes. Two, Four, Six, Eight. They're all still there, all those precious younger ones, all perfect in an unexpected, gentle kind of way. I'm not talking about an idealized version of perfection as in flawless or faultless, more like a mother's version, seeing her Buddha baby in a much bigger body now. I'm talking about the kind of perfection that means there's nothing I would change about my daughter. That's what I'm talking about.

It's already 2011. She'll graduate from high school this year then go off to college in the fall. She'll carry all those younger ones away with her. But she'll come back with older versions of herself, just as lovable, just as kind, just as calm, just as sweet. She'll come back home, to the home of her heart, and find everything is waiting for her. I did.

And when I came home, back to the home of my heart after all that soul-shaking sadness, I found everything waiting for me. And I claimed all those younger versions of myself, even the most difficult, the least perfect. They all live inside me now, content in their togetherness, relaxed and happy, like those ponytail palms.

The following poem by the visionary poet David Whyte seems to capture exactly what I'm talking about—this process of becoming "unutterably" ourselves, accepting all parts of ourselves at all ages, seeing perfection in the seemingly imperfect.

To me, David Whyte's brilliance lies in the way he shines his 1000-watt light on every day things, illuminating the extraordinary in the ordinary. His words remind me to release the misunderstanding or the "great mistake" of my aloneness, coming home to myself and joining in the conversation happening around and through me.

Like the corridor of the moon's light that I saw shining on the water, his words remind me that the light shines on and through everything.

Everything is Waiting for You

Your great mistake is to act the drama
as if you were alone. As if life
were a progressive and cunning crime
with no witness to the tiny hidden
transgressions. To feel abandoned is to deny
the intimacy of your surroundings. Surely,
even you, at times, have felt the grand array;
the swelling presence, and the chorus, crowding
out your solo voice. You must note
the way the soap dish enables you,
or the window latch grants you freedom.
Alertness is the hidden discipline of familiarity.
The stairs are your mentor of things
to come, the doors have always been there
to frighten you and invite you,
and the tiny speaker in the phone
is your dream-ladder to divinity.

Put down the weight of your aloneness
and ease into the conversation.
The kettle is singing even as it pours you
a drink, the cooking pots
have left their arrogant aloofness and
seen the good in you at last. All the birds
and creatures of the world are unutterably
themselves. Everything is waiting for you.

DAVID WHYTE
from *Everything is Waiting for You*
©2003 Many Rivers Press

"The master of the art of living makes little distinction between his work and his play, his labor and his leisure, his mind and his body, his education and his recreation, his love and his religion. He simply pursues his vision of excellence in whatever he does, leaving others to decide whether he is working or playing. To him, he is always doing both."

LAO TZU

CHAPTER 13

REFRAMING ISSUES
AS BLESSINGS

I rarely fight with my teenage daughters, as miraculous as that sounds. Sometimes, I think that most of the energy I had to invest in drama and upset got spent during the two years when I went from married to divorced.

Yesterday, however, that energy reemerged and I had it out with my 13-year-old, Hadley. What caused the argument was saying I would take her shopping, then not wanting to go when the time came.

My hand stops writing as my mind searches for the answer to why I really fought with my daughter. What fear lies beneath the surface that came out as anger?

Ah … Here it is. I see it now as it reemerges—the persistent question: Will I be able to financially support myself and my children?

Yes. That's it. The uncertainty of not knowing. That's what brought all those emotions to the surface yesterday when Hadley wanted to go shopping for a pair of Uggs.

I remember when my dad lost his job after 17 years at the same company. In his autobiography *Only in America,* this is what he wrote about what that was like for him:

———— • ⬬ • ————

"I was 50 years old and had never had to look for a job before, having been recruited by a big eight accounting firm as I graduated from college and then by another company from that accounting firm. Losing my job was very difficult. I went through feelings of inadequacy, anger and concern: Was I really a good executive? Why had this happened to me? What will happen to my family?

Since I had never looked for a job before, I was not sure how to go about doing it. I was fortunate that my company had arranged for me to use the outplacement services of Barbara Crenshaw.

Barbara had her own consulting firm, Crenshaw and Associates, in New York City, helping senior-level executives who had lost their jobs. She helped me get over the emotions of being terminated and laid out a plan for finding the right position. She even helped prepare me for interviews."

———— • ⬬ • ————

I was 27 years old when my dad was 50. I remember going to lunch with my mom and sisters to meet with Barbara so she could get to know our dad through our eyes. She, like my dad, was very good at what she did. Both Barbara and my dad seemed to be masters of the art of living as the ancient Chinese philosopher Lao Tzu so beautifully defined it:

"The master of the art of living makes little distinction between his work and his play, his labor and his leisure, his mind and his body, his education and his recreation, his love and his religion. He simply pursues his vision of excellence in whatever he does, leaving others to decide whether he is working or playing. To him, he is always doing both."

I had one question I had to ask Barbara. It felt very vulnerable, but I was very determined not to leave the restaurant without an answer. When the time came, I gathered all my courage and blurted it out, "Ms. Crenshaw (gulp), is there any chance my dad won't find a new job?"

My dad not having a job was new territory for me since during my lifetime he had only changed jobs once, way back when I was a ten-year-old. Because my dad came home from work singing every day, I knew he loved what he did. I also knew that part of his well-being was tied to his work and the contribution he made through it.

I'll never forget Barbara's matter of fact reply, "Lori, there's only one way your dad won't find a new job. The only way he won't find a new job is if he quits."

Well, what a relief!

After hearing that, all the worry went right out of me. It just disappeared because there was one thing I knew for sure about my dad: He would never quit.

And the same is true for me. Perhaps that's the blessing of having fought with my daughter yesterday, bringing this memory forward and remembering whose daughter I am.

My dad found another job and then another and then another, eventually realizing his dream of being President and CEO of two New York Stock Exchange companies. In his words, "Only in America could a poor kid from the wrong side of the tracks have an opportunity to do the things I have done." My dad grew up poor, very poor, and he made sure we didn't. He never quit.

Supporting myself and my children financially was something I never imagined would be my job. My mom insisted that I, along with my three sisters and my brother, graduate from college, which we all did. My mom was a full-time stay-at-home mom. I imagined I would follow in her footsteps. Never did I entertain the possibility that providing for myself and my daughters would be my responsibility.

The way I saw it, my job was to nurture my girls, raise them, make sure they had everything they needed, just like my mom had done for us. My job was to be at home with them. Supporting us financially was their dad's job. That's the way we had set it up. That's the agreement I thought we had made when I stopped working outside our home, after our first daughter was born.

Supporting myself and my children financially was never my job until it became my job. It's much scarier to carry that responsibility than I ever imagined. And much more rewarding, too.

I spoke recently at my alma mater, the University of Santa Monica, about reframing issues as blessings. I graduated in 2011 from the two-year master's degree program in Spiritual Psychology. Then I graduated again in 2012 from the one-year program known as Consciousness, Health and Healing. And then again in 2013, I graduated from the first ever six-month

Soul-Centered Professional Coaching Program.

My three-and-a-half years at USM can be summed up in two words ... EPIC WIN.

In a TEDtalk, video game designer Jane McGonigal defines an Epic Win as "an outcome so extraordinarily positive that you had no idea it was even possible until you achieved it. It's almost beyond the threshold of imagination and when you get there, you're shocked to discover you're capable of it."

In 2009, when I started at USM, I was a recently divorced, stay-at-home mother of three daughters. When a divorce occurs in the state of California, a mandate immediately goes into effect requiring the non-working spouse to become self-supporting within a certain amount of time. As much as I wanted to be, I was no exception.

Having spent the last 15 years as a mother at home, this mandate terrified me. I had no idea what I could do out in the world or how I would ever find a way of supporting myself and my children.

Well, at USM, I learned how to reframe issues as blessings, discovering the opportunity inherent in whatever is happening. What I discovered about that terrifying mandate was that it was actually working *for* me, not *against* me. That minor change in language created a major shift in perspective inside of me. I realized that without that mandate, I would never have applied to USM and experienced the Epic Wins that were waiting for me there.

Reframing that mandate as a blessing, I also discovered that I don't *have* to become self-supporting, I *get* to become self-supporting. Again, another subtle shift in language created a whole new world of possibilities inside of me. All the worry went right out of me, making my own resolution to success much more manageable and a whole lot more fun. Like Abraham Lincoln said, "Always bear in mind that your own resolution to success is more important than any other one thing."

I ended up going shopping with Hadley yesterday and buying her those Uggs. I also apologized to her for freaking out, for letting my FEAR get the best of me, for Forgetting Everything is All Right (again).

As it turns out, forgetting to reframe issues as blessings can also be a blessing. Eventually, I remembered and offered myself compassion, even forgiveness, for having forgotten momentarily that everything, everything, everything is working for me.

Even fighting with my daughter, then writing about it, turned out to be a blessing. It reminded me that I am currently living beyond the threshold of anything I could have imagined five years ago. And that reminds me that I get to create any future I dare to imagine. Perhaps, I'm modeling for my girls what my dad modeled for me.

South African politician and philanthropist Nelson Mandela said, "There is no joy in settling for a life that is less than the one you are capable of living."

Today I'm a writer, a life coach, a workshop facilitator, a speaker and a mother. Like my dad, I love my work and the contribution I make through it. His commitment to never quitting and to not settling for a life that was less than the one he is capable of living has inspired me to allow my own fear to motivate instead of defeat me, to work for me instead of against me. What a relief.

An Epic Win is:

"an outcome so extraordinarily positive
that you had no idea it was even possible
until you achieved it.
It's almost beyond the threshold
of imagination and when you get there,
you're shocked to discover
you're capable of it."

JANE McGONIGAL

Writing, though, like a labyrinth,

always leads to the center of

whatever it is I'm writing about.

That's the part I'm never certain of,

what the center might be,

where my mind, my heart and my hand

might take me.

CHAPTER 14

COMING HOME

Writer Henry Miller said, "I write to find out what I'm writing about." The same is true for me. I also write to find out what I most need to remember.

Writing is my way of making a deep mental path, thinking over and over the kinds of thoughts I wish to dominate my life. Writing is my way of supporting myself in remembering to let the upside in.

When I write, it feels like walking a pathway in my mind. I stop along that path occasionally, take a look around and record what I see. I write first with a pen in my hand following a pathway of lines on a page. I fill one line after another, snaking my way in straight lines from left to right, back and forth across the page.

But in my mind, the path is never straight. It's a scrolling labyrinth, and I'm never certain where it will lead. Writing, though, like a labyrinth, always leads to the center of whatever it is I'm writing about. That's the part I'm never certain of, what the center might be, where my mind, my heart and my hand might take me.

Scrolling labyrinths remind me of Paris. One of the oldest labyrinths in the world, built in the 1300s, resides inside Chartres Cathedral, 90 kilometers or 56 miles outside of Paris. The labyrinths in Paris aren't as obvious, but they're everywhere. In fact, Paris is recognizable in just about any photo due to this architectural detail—the wrought iron balconies on nearly every building that became labyrinths for me.

I lived in Paris for nine years, and both of the apartments I lived in had beautiful scrolling wrought iron balconies. Having given birth to two of my three daughters in Paris, I would sit on the couch, holding my newborn babies while following with my eyes the black wrought iron path just outside my window.

As I followed the flowing designs of that exquisite wrought iron, what I didn't know at the time was that a blueprint for my writing was being imprinted inside of me. I've never spoken of this before, never. I wonder if anyone will understand. I wonder if anyone will see the scrolling blueprint labyrinths that I saw in those wrought iron balconies.

Before leaving Paris in 2003 and coming home, I went to the flea market at the Porte de Clignancourt and bought five of those balconies. I couldn't leave Paris without them. They went into our container then travelled all the way across the ocean to the port of Los Angeles, arriving a couple months after we did.

I remember leafing through those wrought iron balconies at the flea market one by one, not really knowing what I was looking for. I bought two sets of matching pairs that had been removed from buildings that were being renovated in Paris. I also bought a single one that coordinated with the other four. I thought maybe I'd have them made into tables or just hang them on the wall to remind me of Paris, to get lost in from time to time.

They sat in my California garage for years before I knew what to do with them. The idea came to me while standing in the entrance of my home wondering what could be done with the industrial looking banisters that had been built along with the house in 1978.

I got an estimate for all new banisters which turned out to be way too much. Remembering the wrought iron balconies in my garage, I asked the ironsmith what would be possible working with what we had. Could we incorporate the scrolling wrought iron balconies from Paris into the industrial looking banisters in California?

This is one of my favorite creative hobbies—to take what is and update it, making it better, much better and much more beautiful. I actually love the "constraints" of working with what's already there. I love the challenge of winding my way through to the beauty, landing in the center, up-leveling everything.

So the ironsmith took the existing banisters and incorporated the wrought iron balconies I had shipped home from Paris. The feature I least liked about my home, those old industrial banisters, transformed into one of the features I like best. This transformation happened just by taking what is, working with what I already had, imagining what might be possible. And it cost me a whole lot less than the estimate for all new banisters.

What I'm aware of as I'm describing updating my banisters is that I'm also describing the process I take my clients through as a life coach.

We take what is (who they believe themselves to be) and

transform it simply by seeing the possibilities and replacing outdated assumptions and beliefs with something new, something more beautiful. And updating their inner worlds often creates transformation in their outer worlds as well.

Ramanuja, an 11th century Hindu theologian and philosopher, said, "What we seek as our highest goal depends upon what we believe ourselves to be."

People transform. I've seen it over and over. As we reframe and refine our lives, we up-level in the most remarkable ways. We end up in places and with lives we never dreamed of when we were caught in our outdated assumptions that we are our personalities, stuck with ourselves as we are.

Here's the truth … We are never stuck. Not forever, anyway. Stuck simply defined is living untrue assumptions as if they were true. Even assumptions or beliefs about ourselves that seem really solid, like my 1978 bannisters, can be updated, made more beautiful. Anything is possible. Our outer world reminds us of this all the time. Things transform and get better, sometimes much, much better. And so can we. All that's required is a simple updating of who and what we believe ourselves to be.

This following quote from C.S. Lewis in *Mere Christianity* beautifully illustrates this process:

———————— • ◆ • ————————

"Imagine yourself as a living house. God comes in to rebuild that house. At first, perhaps, you can understand what He is doing. He is getting the drains right and stopping the leaks in the roof and so on; you knew that those jobs needed doing and so you are not surprised. But presently He starts knocking the house about in a way that hurts abominably and does not seem to make any sense. What on earth is He up to? The explanation is that He is building quite a different house from the one you thought of—throwing out a new wing here, putting on an extra floor there, running up towers, making courtyards. You thought you were being made into a decent little cottage: but He is building a palace. He intends to come and live in it Himself."

One of my clients is in the middle of this process. I just received an email from her saying that she'd asked for a separation from her husband. She's very intentional about this time apart, this reconstruction. It takes courage to construct or reconstruct our lives in such a way that we live well inside the homes of our hearts as individuals and as couples.

She wants to explore how to make improvements in the home of her own heart, and then see what happens. She's scared and longs to move back into the familiar, the comfortable inner home that she knew before the reconstruction began. But she's clear that although it "hurts abominably," she doesn't want the same life she's had.

And she's not stuck. She's free to update, up-level, rebuild, transform. We all are. We've just forgotten or we've let moving into the uncomfortableness of the unfamiliar stop us.

I don't know what will happen with my client. I admire her courage to step into the unknown, to up-level her life and possibly her marriage. Sometimes we have to separate from what is in order to build something more beautiful.

C.S. Lewis' quote and my client's marriage remind me of

the older homes in my neighborhood. These homes are called "tear downs" by some and "fixer uppers" by others. They can be either or both. There isn't a right way or a wrong way to think about them. There's simply a question to be answered. It's the same question God seems to be asking in that C.S. Lewis quote, and my client is asking about her marriage: What can be done?

That question makes me think of my favorite part in another C.S. Lewis book, *The Lion, The Witch and The Wardrobe.* Peter, Susan, Lucy and the two beavers finally reach the Stone Table and meet Aslan. Mr. Beaver has to explain to Aslan that Edmund has betrayed them and joined the White Witch, and Aslan assures everyone that all will be done to rescue Edmund.

It makes me cry every time. What can be done? All will be done to rescue one soul. All will be done. Why? Because one soul, every soul, carries such beauty, such value, such worth.

Sometimes, we have to get lost in the labyrinth before we see this, before we experience ourselves as beautiful, valuable and worthy. Sometimes, we have to "imagine ourselves as living houses" and allow ourselves to be reconstructed. And like Edmund, sometimes, we have to join the White Witch of addiction or other destructive patterns before we see the truth of who we are and update outdated assumptions about who and what we believe ourselves to be.

We can live in heaven on earth if we have the eyes to see it. If we have the eyes to see our own beauty, value and worth, then we'll see that all is being done to bring us home, home to live with God in the center of our very own hearts.

People transform.

I've seen it over and over.

As we reframe and refine our lives,

we up-level in the most remarkable ways.

We end up in places and with lives

we never dreamed of when we were caught

in our outdated assumptions

that we are our personalities,

stuck with ourselves as we are.

I no longer bully myself
into some form of compliance.
I neither hide nor feel ashamed
of my vulnerability.
I don't buy into the misunderstanding
that my light could ever be extinguished,
that the embers of love could ever burn out.
I no longer stomp around my consciousness
making threatening demands.

CHAPTER 15

D'Artagnan and The Three Musketeers

Random memories about my life as a little girl spring unbidden into my mind today. My mom had salt and pepper shakers, plastic ones, salt was yellow and pepper was green. She used them every day. I can still see her hands holding them as she sprinkled first the salt and then the pepper on whatever she was cooking. Unlike me, she is a very good cook.

She doesn't have those shakers anymore, but she had them for years. I mean like over 30 years. And a green plastic colander. With five kids, she made lots of spaghetti in that colander. I'm seeing the beauty in ordinary things today, things we take for granted, like salt and pepper shakers, moms and colanders.

One of the things I took for granted was being with my children every Christmas. I'm away from them every other Christmas now. This is our eighth year and my fourth Christmas without them.

I remember the first one, Christmas 2007. My girls are young, ages thirteen, ten and five. I'm determined to send them off with a smile, determined not to let them see my broken-hearted terror of getting through this first Christmas or any Christmas without them.

It's Friday, December 21. They will go with their dad for the whole week. I won't see them again until Sunday, December 30. That's how we set up custody over the holidays. If they're with me for Thanksgiving, they go with him for Christmas, and I get them for New Year's. The next year, we do the reverse.

It's late when the girls get in his car and pull away into a life I know little about. I crawl beneath the covers, finally letting the tears have their way with me. My optimism, the very thing I believed to be inextinguishable, my best quality, has disappeared. I cannot find even a flicker of it inside me. And without that light, I cannot see how I will ever make it to the other side of December 25. That date, 4 days in the future, looms large before me, blocking my view of anything beyond it.

I cannot see how I will survive. I cannot see above the massive wave of emotion that has me in its wretched grip now and is waiting for me even more fiercely on Christmas Day. It will surely bury me beneath its watery, airless brutality.

This is it. This is what finally destroys me, forces the air out of my lungs, leaving me utterly lifeless. My certainty around this is astounding. There is no way I'll emerge on December 26. There is no December 26 for me this year. There are only the raging waters of my own emotions that I cannot control, waiting wickedly for me on Christmas.

I cry myself to sleep or almost to sleep anyway. Right before sleep casts its sweet spell, I hear three words. It's like they've come galloping on horseback from far away, determined to get to me before sleep does. I'm too tired and too close to the unconscious world to drag myself out and write them down. I'm seconds away from thoughtless oblivion. So I ask whoever is listening, whoever is on those horses, to remind me in the morning. "Please," I say, "please, whoever you are. Remind me in the morning."

The horses stop suddenly, just before the line that separates the conscious world from the unconscious world. The three riders dismount effortlessly, quickly and say before I fade away from them, "Remember DDB. Just remember the first letter of each word, DDB. DDB. DDB. Remember. We may not be here in the morning."

Before seeing them slip away, before the blackout curtain of unconsciousness closes, I imprint these letters inside me, insisting that this acronym assist me in remembering the wisdom in their words, the meaningful message of these riders.

I sleep. In the morning, I wake, remembering the letters easily, without a clue as to what the words might be.

"Ugh! Really?! Come on brain! Remember!" I demand as I try with all my might to draw them up from the depths of wherever they're hiding. I stomp around inside my consciousness, throwing my arms in the air, looking everywhere for those three words, those three simple words spoken by those horsemen that brought comfort, peace and sleep.

"Forget it! They're gone. I told you. You will never make it. You won't survive this," some bully inside of me sneers.

I start packing. I've been invited to spend Christmas with my boyfriend and his two boys in Arizona. I actually feel a bit sorry for them. They have no idea what they're in for. This morning, I wince at their kindness and the unsuspecting way they've extended this invitation to me, a crazy woman who can't even remember three simple words and who certainly can't do anything except let the relentless hurricane of her emotions completely destroy her and Christmas. Poor guys.

I shrug my shoulders and keep packing, muttering to myself, blaming my ex-husband for all that's wrong with the world. It has to be somebody's fault. It might as well be his. There's lots of deep sighing and seemingly insurmountable sadness, leaden feet and slumped shoulders.

"What difference does it make? You won't be here after Christmas anyway. You're not coming back. This is it. You won't survive this." There's that bully again. That smug, condescending inner voice scares me, convinces me.

I'm on my way to the airport, sitting in the backseat of a taxi, when I remember the words. The three words spring unbidden into my mind from that place where I had stored them the night before. I check them using the acronym DDB. Yep, they work. It's them, those same three words that the horsemen brought.

I recognize who those men on horses are now. I didn't see it last night, but I see it now. The Three Musketeers. That's who rescued me from my made-up misery. They seem to be standing before me on the movie screen of my mind, smiling and looking bashfully down at their boots, having been recognized. They are unmistakable in their broad brimmed hats, brassy buttoned coats and dusty brown leather boots riding high above their knees.

I smile, experiencing again the blessing of their coming. Slowly, I repeat the words over and over. They're mine now, those words. I close my eyes, lean my head back against the seat and keep smiling. I nod in silent gratitude to each of these brave Musketeers who came from the great out there to deliver their glad tidings of great joy to me this Christmas. Maybe I will make it through December 25 to the 26th and even beyond. Maybe. I feel the embers of what I thought had been extinguished begin to stir inside me.

The Three Musketeers is a book written by a Frenchman, Alexandre Dumas, way back in the 19th century. It's the story of a young man, D'Artagnan, who in 1625 leaves his home to travel to Paris to join the Musketeers of the Guard. He makes three friends, Athos, Porthos and Aramis, and together they live by the motto: "All for one, one for all." I don't have any particular memory of reading this book. Like other random memories, it seems to have sprung unbidden into my mind, right when I needed it.

Perhaps those Musketeers rode across all those centuries to find me that Friday night in 2007, reaching me right when I needed them. They certainly seem to live by their own motto as well as the words they gave me, the words that rescued me. I like to imagine that D'Artagnan might have sent them. What I know for sure is that they appeared right before I fell asleep, each with a word to offer me.

Here they are … Here are those words that Athos, Porthos and Aramis rode across time to give me … *Don't Decide Before* (DDB). Those were their words, their gifts that they handed to me like gold, frankincense and myrrh.

Don't Decide Before.

There were no tears on Christmas, no uncontrollable emotional breakdowns. I made it through. We all did. It was lovely and sweet, even though it was different from any other Christmas, for all of us.

Today, many years after that first Christmas away from my girls, I no longer pretend to know what will happen or demand that I should know what will happen. I no longer bully myself into some form of compliance. I neither hide nor feel ashamed of my vulnerability. I don't buy into the misunderstanding that my light could ever be extinguished, that the embers of love could ever burn out. I no longer stomp around my consciousness making threatening demands. I don't even blame my ex for all that's wrong with the world anymore. Instead, I live by the new motto those Three Musketeers brought: *I Don't Decide Before.*

My Three Musketeers: McCall, Hadley and Madison

I smile, experiencing again the blessing of their coming. Slowly, I repeat the words over and over. They're mine now, those words. I close my eyes, lean my head back against the seat and keep smiling. I nod in silent gratitude to each of these brave Musketeers who came from the great out there to deliver their glad tidings of great joy.

Astronomer Carl Sagan said,
"We are a way for the cosmos
to know itself."
In other words, as we look through
the lens of the spiritual consciousness,
we are a way for love to know itself.
And letting the upside in
is a way of attuning to
and aligning with love.

CHAPTER 16

LETTING THE UPSIDE IN

It's January, and we're in the middle of another warm, sunny day in Southern California. It's heaven really, not just the weather, but the California lifestyle—the openness, the gentle way of being, the expansion. I'm sure the weather influences it. We smile at each other, rubbing our arms to warm them, and say, "It's freezing!" when it's 49 degrees outside.

The weather isn't the only upside to living in California. It's just an ongoing reminder that there's always an upside. To wake up in January to the soft, warm air helps me remember to look for the upside, to recognize the positive, favorable or advantageous aspect, to find the promise and potential in everything.

There's even an upside to divorce. There, I said it. I didn't know it then, when I chose divorce, but I know it now. I only saw divorce then as the worst possible thing that could happen to an individual or a family. But it's not true. There's an upside to divorce, too. It's what no one ever told me about, the upside. I heard plenty about the downside and absolutely nothing about the up.

The truth is, when I was safely tucked into my marriage, even if I'd heard anything about the upside, I couldn't really have heard it. I was too busy doing everything right. Not really. I was just busy thinking that I was doing everything right, trying to convince myself and everyone else that I was lovable.

What a relief to be released from the tyranny of my own thoughts, the mistaken certainty that I had *to do* something in order *to be* lovable. That's the upside to divorce, the upward movement or trend. I learned another way of being—a more open, a gentler, a more expansive way.

It's like what writer Max Ehrmann said, "Whether or not it is clear to you, no doubt the universe is unfolding as it should." The universe is constantly supporting us in seeing the upside, in experiencing life as the gift and blessing that it is, in seeing the potential for gain in everything. Most of us don't have to experience divorce to get this, but I did.

Even though I was convinced that my ex had ruined my life, he didn't. He sort of saved it. Well, I can't give him all the credit, but he probably does deserve some. Looking back, I see it all went the way it needed to go for our highest good. Even though it wasn't at all clear to me at the time, the universe was unfolding exactly as it should.

Our song, "Little Wing" by Sting, the song my ex chose for us, tells most of the story. The first 40 years of my life, I spent walking through the clouds, co-dependently letting others take anything they wanted from me. The lyrics go something like that, but I added the co-dependent part, of course.

Our song brings the lyrics of another Sting song to mind. In "I Was Brought to My Senses," one of the lines goes like this, "The wounds he gave me were the wounds that would heal me." That's the truth. The wounds he gave me were the wounds that healed me. I'm no longer walking through the clouds. The gravity of what happened grounds me to the earth now. And instead of letting others take anything they want from me, I'm keeping some of me for myself. Today, I keep some of me for me. Now, I'm my own good company.

In the past, I had to distract myself to escape being alone with myself and my ongoing demand for perfection. Now, when my girls are with their dad and I'm alone, I feel blessed, not abandoned. And there's no longer any demand for perfection.

Therein lies the great paradox of aloneness. Sometimes it takes time alone to discover just how supported we are. We have to be alone in order to experience that we are never really alone. The unseen world is real, always offering us ongoing support. I had to spend time on my own, alone, to see this. That's part of the upside too, experiencing the blessing of my aloneness.

I love the 26 days a month that I spend raising my three brown-eyed daughters. And I love the four days a month when they're with their dad. To hold both as blessings seems like a blessing itself.

There's something about holding both as blessings, something illusory and evasive that wants to be caught, discovered, revealed. We hold both of just about everything: joy and sorrow, laughter and tears, love and hate, softness and hardness, lightness and darkness. To see both as blessings, that's been the challenge.

I remember being invited to a party after completing the first year of my master's program at USM. The day of the party the hostess's well-loved dog was killed in a kennel fire. I thought for sure she would cancel the party, but she didn't. Instead, we held both the sorrow of her losing her dog and the joy of our successful completion of first year together that night.

It can be done. Most of us are doing it daily, not even aware of the depth we ourselves contain. The fluidity of our bodies allows for it. Being 65% water, we're able to contain much, just like the ocean.

The ocean expands to hold all kinds of things, sometimes revealing itself to us by what washes up on shore. Like the ocean, we expand too. And like the ocean, we have no maximum capacity. We too are great containers of life and all its duality. The ocean fluidly and easily expands, making room for everything that enters, including us. We walk into the ocean and become one with it. It wraps itself around us as well as everything else, like love.

Today, the ocean inspires me to walk in and let love wrap itself around me. It also inspires me to wrap myself around love. Instead of filtering my life through some obscure, distorted, impersonal perspective that not even I can identify with, I see that life is personal. My life is, anyway. And like the ocean, I contain all of it.

For me, being divorced allows me to live outside the crushing judgment and constant demand for perfection. What I'm aware of is this ... No one did that to me. I did that to myself. I was the one with the crushing judgments of me and the constant demands for perfection. No one did that to me, except me.

There's still anger that comes up sometimes because things didn't go the way I thought they should. But I don't choose to go there very often anymore. It's not very interesting to stay in anger. It's the same thing day after day.

Wonder is way better. I wonder now what I was so afraid of then. Why was I so afraid of containing life in all its opposites?

Why was I so afraid to hold married and divorced as the blessings they both are? Why did I put myself to sleep, then stay there for so long, mistakenly thinking life had to be this way or that way, not both? Perhaps I thought I couldn't handle it or I couldn't expand to hold it all.

I don't condemn myself for any of this. I just wonder. I think what really allowed me to overcome the fear of containing all of it was realizing that everything has an upside, that the universe is unfolding exactly as it should.

Astronomer Carl Sagan said, "We are a way for the cosmos to know itself." In other words, as we look through the lens of the spiritual consciousness, we are a way for love to know itself. And letting the upside in is a way of attuning to and aligning with love.

It's like watching Elton John play the piano. If you've ever seen him play, you know what I'm talking about. He becomes one with that instrument. The music coming through Elton John is a way for the piano to know itself. Whether he's playing the piano or the piano is playing him, it's almost impossible to tell, the oneness is so complete.

I woke up to oneness when I was ready, and it was worth the wait. I discovered that I had been and am being held in love, that love not only wraps itself around me like the ocean, but I, like the ocean, wrap myself around love. I also discovered that, like the ocean, I hold an entire sea of experience inside of me.

After nearly 50 years on the earth, I contain much and lots of treasures have washed up on my shore. I pick them up one by one, examining them, and remembering, there's always an upside if I'm willing to let it in. It's quite beautiful really, like the weather in Southern California—open, gentle, expansive.

She releases her grip on a bottom rung

and ascends right on up that ladder.

She remembers what it feels like to be

creative, imaginative, funny and loving.

In other words,

she remembers what it feels like to live well.

And living well aligns her with something

that not living well never will.

It aligns her with love,

where she discovers the truth of who she is —

owner of her own destiny.

CHAPTER 17

SAVING MS. TRAVERS

Today, I want to write about the ladder of consciousness, self-acceptance, self-compassion and self-forgiveness. I want to explore the idea that anything that has happened that we think should not have happened keeps us in a victim position at the bottom of the ladder, keeps us from living well, keeps us from cooperating with what is, or in other words, keeps us from rising up the ladder and being owners of our own destinies.

I first heard about the ladder of consciousness from my coach Steve Chandler. He taught me to use this imaginary ladder as a tool to determine where I am in my own consciousness at any given time.

When I'm living at the top of the ladder, I'm filled with creativity, imagination, compassion, humor and love. And great things happen from up there. At the bottom of the ladder, however, I'm filled with fear, anger, worry, resentment and upset. And not much at all happens from down there.

It was a game changer when I learned that as humans our natural state of being is at the top of the ladder. In fact, the universe rushes to support us when filled with a sense of our own aliveness. And unexpectedly, it takes a lot less energy and a lot less effort to reside at the top of the ladder than it does to live at the bottom.

Here's why … In order to keep ourselves at the bottom of the ladder, we have to continuously engage in negative self-talk, telling ourselves stories meant to sabotage and restrict. That takes a whole lot of energy and a whole lot of effort, too. But, when residing at the top of the ladder, we get to relax and come into resonance with the beautiful truth of who we are—creative, imaginative, compassionate, humorous, loving beings.

There's something about writing that shifts my perspective, moving me from a victim of circumstance to an owner of my own destiny. And once I've become the owner, I move to the top of the ladder where I relax and everything gets easier and more fun.

Cooperating with what is gets easier from our natural state of well-being at the top of the ladder. It's much easier to experience the gifts and blessings of life from the top of the ladder too. And we can take ourselves up there anytime we want.

One of the best examples I've seen of this lately is in the Disney film *Saving Mr. Banks*. Ms. Travers, brilliantly played by Emma Thompson, is a woman who travels from the bottom to the top of the ladder. She does this by letting go of the misunderstanding that her childhood should have been different than it was and that she or her parents should have been different than they were. As Walt Disney, beautifully played by Tom Hanks, says at the end of film, "Aren't you tired of remembering it that way? Don't you want to finish the story and have a life that isn't dictated by the past?"

As Ms. Travers is writing the screenplay for *Mary Poppins* with the creative team at Disney, she rewrites her own life story, too. She replaces whatever thoughts are keeping her at the bottom of the ladder with new thoughts that take her right up to the top. She learns the difference between stubbornly clinging to the past, demanding that it be the way she remembers it and gently releasing her grip, allowing new possibilities to emerge. Standing back, seeing her life from a new perspective, allows Ms. Travers to receive the gifts and blessings from her past, claiming the unclaimed treasures of her childhood.

One of the gifts and blessings that came from and through Ms. Travers' seemingly difficult childhood is the beloved character Mary Poppins. Ms. Travers could not have created that character if her life had unfolded any differently than it did. So living at the top of the ladder is also about coming to peace with the past, collecting the gifts and blessings of whatever the past holds in service to living well now.

Reframing. That's the technical word for it. It often requires that we look through a different lens than the one we habitually look through. But it's always possible and anyone can do it. Mary Poppins does this with Jane and Michael Banks; and it's exactly what Ms. Travers eventually does for herself when she travels to California and begins collaborating with Disney.

It's really about taking what is or what was and allowing it to work *for* us instead of *against* us, looking for the opportunities and blessings in every challenging situation. It's not hard, but it can be uncomfortable, especially if we've attached to just one interpretation of events or can only see one perspective.

Steve Chandler says it this way, "Life is like a movie with many endings. Give me any situation in your life, anything, and I'll ask you one question: Given what you just told me, what would you like to create?"

We get to write and rewrite, frame and reframe every ending based on what we're willing to create. Self-acceptance, self-compassion and self-forgiveness, those are the inner practices that allow us to rewrite and reframe, moving us from the bottom to the top of the ladder. That's another thing Ms. Travers does in the film. She shifts her perspective from one of resistance, constriction and stubbornness to one of creativity, expansion and resourcefulness.

The following quote is from both movies, *Mary Poppins* and *Saving Mr. Banks*, "Wind's in the east, mist coming in like something is brewing, about to begin. I can't put my finger on what lies in store, but I feel what's to happen all happened before."

Mary Poppins comes to the rescue twice, not to save Ms. Travers' father, Mr. Banks, but to save Ms. Travers herself, first as a child, then again, much later in life, as an adult. And Ms. Travers, after a great deal of resistance, constriction and stubbornness, finally lets her in, allowing Mary Poppins to uplift and inspire her, receiving the real blessing of her coming and claiming the treasures of her childhood.

Steven Pressfield, author of *The War of Art*, said, "The more important an activity is to your soul's evolution, the more resistance you'll feel." He defines resistance as "the negative force that arises whenever we try to move from a lower level to a higher level." In other words, resistance is what happens when we start to move up the rungs of the ladder of consciousness from the bottom to the top.

Ms. Travers begins her ascent when she starts to focus on what she gets to create now, letting go of what she thought happened and her very young interpretation of it. She reframes her past, accepts it (all of it) in a larger, more beautiful, more complete context. She forgives herself and others, then starts tapping her foot, dancing and singing. She smiles, really smiles for the first time in years, allowing compassion for herself to finally surface.

She releases her grip on a bottom rung and ascends right on up that ladder. She remembers what it feels like to be creative, imaginative, funny and loving. In other words, she remembers what it feels like to live well. And living well aligns her with something that not living well never will. It aligns her with love, where she discovers the truth of who she is—owner of her own destiny.

Walt Disney's words to Ms. Travers finally set her free, "George Banks will be honored. George Banks will be redeemed. George Banks and all he stands for will be saved. Maybe not in life but in imagination. It's what we storytellers do—we restore order with imagination. We instill hope, again and again and again." Ms. Travers finally receives what she had given all those who read her stories about Mary Poppins—hope.

I wonder sometimes if what's happening in any given moment is more beautiful, more inspiring, more uplifting than anything we've allowed ourselves to imagine. What if what's happening this very moment in our lives, every moment of our lives, is happening *for us*, not *to us*?

This subtle shift inside moves us out of resistance, constriction and stubbornness and into creativity, expansion and resourcefulness. We automatically move up the ladder and our lives automatically improve even in areas that seem unrelated. Everything gets better.

This possibility coming through me today is a gentle one, not a way of judging ourselves or demanding that things be different than they are. Instead, what if we were to ask ourselves, gently and with great love, "If this were happening *for me*, not *to me*, what would be the blessing or opportunity in it?" And what if that simple question allowed us to gracefully cooperate with what is, moving us right on up the ladder and into love?

Sometimes, the answers to these questions don't come immediately. When they don't, it may be an opportunity to further align with the benevolent universe, to see God as a loving being no matter what's happening in our lives, to see ourselves as loving beings, too, no matter what's happening. It may be an opportunity to practice self-acceptance, self-compassion and self-forgiveness.

Sometimes, we can't see the learning, we can't see how whatever is happening is serving us until we move through it and look back from the other side. This reminds me of something Ernest Hemingway wrote, "Maybe away from Paris I could write about Paris as in Paris I could write about Michigan. I did not know it was too early for that because I did not know Paris well enough."

Sometimes, we can't see what's happening until we're on the other side of it, until we can look back from someplace else, another vantage point. Sometimes, it's too early, and we have to wait to see the learning until we know whatever's happening well enough. And sometimes, "what's to happen all happened before." Our patterns tend to repeat themselves, occurring again and again until we collect the treasures and begin living well now.

What sees us through, what allows us to collect the gifts and blessings from the past and present, is holding in the possibility and eventually the knowing that whatever is happening is serving our highest good, experiencing that we really do live in a benevolent universe. It's asking ourselves and answering the question, "Given what is, what would I like to create?" It's writing and rewriting, framing and reframing until we restore ourselves to our natural state of well-being. It's allowing what is to work for us instead of against us. It's that subtle shift, that gentle reframe that restores order, moving us from the bottom of the ladder to the top, transforming us from disillusioned victims to creative owners of our own destinies.

Perhaps the universe asks us

all day every day,

"What do you need from me?

How can I serve you?"

Imagine the universe wanting

to give us what we need, to serve us.

Once my own creation started to take form,

I wanted to serve it,

I wanted it to have everything it needed.

CHAPTER 18

GOD'S MASTERPIECES

I'm looking at the visioning board I did a couple of years ago when I knew it was time to write. Before beginning my first book about what it was like living abroad on 9/11, I created this writer's collage.

There's a wonderful book by Lucia Capacchione called *Visioning*. I carefully followed her guidance while creating this collage, this visioning board that she calls "a kind of storyboard or blueprint of the life you want to create, a wish map." She wrote, "Visioning is a process for creating the life you want. It is a method for finding the dream that lives in your heart and translating it into the world of three dimensions."

In my writer's collage, I included a picture of a man who's wading through flood waters that reach all the way up to his chin. High above his head, he's holding notebooks filled with papers. I remember gluing him onto the page because when I saw him, I became consciously aware of a dream that I had been holding in my heart for many years. I dreamed of one day writing something that would be worth saving.

That's what I love about Capacchione's visioning process. It's not just about what we *think* we want. It's also about bypassing our rational minds and allowing our hearts to make themselves known. As we glue onto the page images and words that resonate and that cause our hearts to pound, we have an inner experience of animation and excitement.

Capacchione writes, "In visioning, we are reshaping the images of our heads to catch up with the vision in our hearts. When we stop concentrating on our outer situation and pay attention to our inner vision, we create the world as we wish it to be. And we participate in divine creation. This is how the Creator works through us if we will allow it."

Writer Martha Beck has been one of my heroes for many years. I've read most of her books, and I always flip to her article first in O *Magazine* to read what she's written. It's always good.

On this writer's collage, right here next to me, there's a quote from Martha Beck that I cut out of O *Magazine,* "Real power is usually unspectacular, a simple setting aside of fear that allows the free flow of love. But it changes everything."

I participated in a workshop recently based on the book *The Artist's Way.* It was written by another one of my heroes, Julia Cameron. I hadn't done any art in many years aside from my collages. Yet when Helen Bradley, my inspiring instructor, put materials in front of me, I created something. I set aside any fear that came up and focused instead on what she placed before me. My curiosity about what might get created carried me right on through to the other side.

Helen taught me how to create what wanted to come into form by asking questions of my art like, "What do you need from me? How can I serve you?" Then once whatever wanted to be created came into form, Helen taught me to ask it, "Who are you? And what message do you have to share with me?"

This possibility had never occurred to me before—to ask my art what it needed from me, how I could serve it. I wonder if that's what the universe does.

Perhaps the universe asks us all day every day, "What do you need from me? How can I serve you?" Imagine the universe wanting to give us what we need, to serve us. Once my own creation started to take form, I wanted to serve it, I wanted it to have everything it needed.

And what about the universe asking us the questions, "Who are you? What message do you have to share with me today?" Answering those questions certainly gives the universe a lot of information about us and who and what we believe ourselves to be. I've asked the universe these very same questions for years. But it didn't occur to me until Helen's workshop that the universe might be asking them of me, too, as a child of creation, as God's art, as one of His seven billion masterpieces.

Dr. Mary Hulnick designed a very simple, very sweet, guided meditation that supports the setting aside of fear and the free flow of love by seeing through the eyes of the soul. It also very clearly answers the question that the universe may be asking, "Who are you?"

This meditation offers such a beautiful way of answering that question that with Mary's permission, I've included it. Mary says a sentence then invites those listening to repeat the sentence. As we repeat these sentences, we give ourselves and the universe a whole lot of information about us and about who and what we believe ourselves to be, opening the door for all kinds of new possibilities to emerge.

A Meditation of the Soul

Who am I?
Who am I?

I am a center of pure loving awareness.
I am a center of pure loving awareness.

I have a body and I am more than my body.
I have a body and I am more than my body.

I have a mind and I am more than my mind.
I have a mind and I am more than my mind.

I have emotions and I am more than my emotions.
I have emotions and I am more than my emotions.

I observe how my body, mind and emotions experience the gift of life.
I observe how my body, mind and emotions experience the gift of life.

And I am learning from this experience.
And I am learning from this experience.

I am learning that my true nature is loving.
I am learning that my true nature is loving.

Who am I?
Who am I?
I am a center of pure loving awareness.
I am a center of pure loving awareness.

And I am always at peace.
And I am always at peace.

As centers of pure loving awareness, it makes perfect sense that love flows freely through the universe and into us, God's masterpieces. Aligning with who we truly are and setting aside our fears connects us to that eternal well-spring of loving, our true nature, where we are always at peace.

And what Capacchione writes about visioning also serves our natural state of wellness, "Let me remind you that the whole idea of mistakes is a myth. There is no such thing. There is no right way or wrong way to do any of this work."

When we look through soul-centered eyes or the lens of the spiritual consciousness, we see that life is all about learning. Setting aside any misunderstandings or fears about the mistakes we think we made in the past or the ones we might make in the future is a step into real power.

By allowing the universe to serve us as children of creation, as God's art and as God's masterpieces, we become more and more aware of the truth of who and what we are, centers of pure loving awareness. That's a step into real power, a setting aside of fear that allows the free flow of love. And, like Martha Beck said, that changes everything.

I was born to do what I'm doing.
I know this by the graceful way
these practices have unfolded,
with so much gentle guidance and
ongoing assistance from Spirit.
Today, I'm living the dream that
resides in my heart.

CHAPTER 19

I Didn't Know I Knew

I t's 1996. I'm living in Paris, France. Sarah Ban Breathnach's book *Simple Abundance* arrives at my door. A gift to me, a 30-year-old ex-pat, a wife and a mother of two young daughters.

Sarah begins with the words of Willa Cather, "She heard a deeper vibration, a kind of echo, of all that the writer said, and did not say." Prophetic words really, with Sarah Ban Breathnach as the writer and me, Lori Cash Richards, hearing the deeper vibration of her words. *Simple Abundance* kept me company for many years. That book, Sarah's words, turned out to be such good company.

Fast forward 17 years …

It's 2013. I'm living in Palos Verdes, California. Sarah's lovely face appears on my computer screen, Oprah's Super Soul Sunday. Another gift to me, now a 48-year-old writer and life coach, a single mother of three nearly grown daughters.

Sarah talks about keeping a promise she made to herself by buying shoes—multiple pairs of Manolo Blahniks in London. And I remember a promise I made to myself, too. I wrote this promise into a poem so I wouldn't forget.

The Promise: I Will Do This, But Not Forever

I didn't know I knew
until I knew,
I know exactly what I'm doing.

This knowing,
neither arrogant nor antagonistic,
is the promise made long ago,
in a world no longer visible
except in those secret moments
of knowing.

I didn't know I knew
until I knew,
I know exactly what I'm doing.

I've made up all kinds of stories
about what happened and why
and who's to blame.

But here I am,
seeing myself
as I am.

I see that being me
has to do with me,
not anyone else.

I was in a hurry to get married,
or so it seemed.
At 23, I said yes,
even before
the sealer was done speaking.

But the truth is,
I was in no hurry
to get married.

I was in a hurry
to get back to being me,
and it took me nearly 20 years.

Somehow,
through grace or luck or determination,
I became more of me by getting married.

I made promises
to the man I married,
but I made promises to myself first.

I promised me that
I will do this, but not forever.

In the end,
he couldn't compete
with what I promised me.

If I'd known, maybe
I should have told him,
But, like I said …

I didn't know I knew
until I knew,
I know exactly what I'm doing.

After divorcing in 2007, I began to reinvent myself, graduating with honors from the University of Santa Monica in 2011, 2012 and 2013. Now, I'm putting all those degrees to work as a writer, a life coach, a workshop facilitator and a speaker.

That part of me who knows exactly what I'm doing loves to speak with that part of my clients who knows exactly what they're doing. We explore together questions like: *What is it you want? Why do you want this? What's the goal beneath the goal or what's the inner experience you're really after? Deep down, at the purest level of knowing, what is it you really want to create?*

I was born to do what I'm doing. I know this by the graceful way these practices have unfolded, with so much gentle guidance and ongoing assistance from Spirit. Today, I'm living the dream that resides in my heart. Now, I assist others in exploring who they are, in finding the dreams that reside in their hearts and discovering how to make those dreams their reality. We look through the eyes of love and see how they, like me, know exactly what they're doing.

One way we experience who we are and access the dreams that reside in our hearts is through a process I learned at USM called identifying, owning and accepting projections.

In Drs. Ron and Mary Hulnick's words, here's the opportunity inherent in projections:

———— • ◆ • ————

"As one pursues the path of growth, the defense mechanism of projection can be challenging whether one is dealing with disowning of the 'negative' or 'positive' within oneself. The challenge of acknowledging, owning and accepting 'negative' projections are apparent. Similarly, the disowning of the best within us allows us to maintain unworthiness, dependency, helplessness, and of course, anger associated with disempowering ourselves. Identifying, owning and accepting projections also involves a willingness to accept responsibility for the best in us. It means letting go of the comfort zone of denial of ourselves as loving human beings."

———————————•——————————

Again, Willa Cather's words capture the subtleness of this process, "She heard a deeper vibration, a kind of echo, of all that the writer said, and did not say." I go with my clients into their inner worlds where we hear, with the ears of our hearts, that "deeper vibration, a kind of echo," of all that the client says and does not say. We explore that comfort zone of denial and release the judgments we've placed against ourselves, eventually accepting responsibility for the best within us.

Brenda Ueland, author of *If You Want to Write*, described this process beautifully, "Listening is a magnetic and strange thing, a creative force. When people really listen to each other in a quiet, fascinated attention, the creative fountain inside each of us begins to spring and cast up new thoughts and unexpected wisdom."

Let me give you an example. I was going through my client notes this week and came across a lovely positive projection that one of my clients shared with me. He didn't recognize it as a positive projection at the time, only later when I pointed it out to him. Positive projections are like that.

We don't always recognize the best within ourselves. But when we're willing to listen to ourselves and each other with "quiet, fascinated attention," then we discover that projections hold the deeper vibrations of who we really are. That might be the echo Willa Cather was talking about.

My client Marcus was going through a tough time. He was being very hard on himself, critical, demanding and unkind. He mentioned a friend whom he respected very much so I asked Marcus what he admired in his friend.

This is what he said, "He's a solid guy who loves everyone without judging anyone. He likes himself; he's comfortable in his own skin. He's a devoted, loving husband and friend. He loves where he is in his life; he's found a sense of peace. He's humble while being wildly successful."

There's the goal beneath the goal for my client, the inner experience he was really after. He wanted to experience the best version of himself, the one he was projecting onto his friend. Deep down, at the purest level of knowing, what Marcus was saying about his friend was what Marcus wanted to create in his own life.

Writer and educator Parker Palmer said, "The best way to make sure that my questions will welcome the soul is to ask them with an honest open spirit. And the best way to cultivate that spirit is to remind myself regularly that everyone has an inner teacher whose authority in his or her life far exceeds my own." That inner teacher is the part of us who knows exactly what we're doing, even when we think we don't.

I gently reminded Marcus that he could not see these qualities in his friend if each one of them didn't already exist inside of him. He would not recognize them. He simply would not/could not see them. Somewhere in him knew this.

"Our deepest wishes are whispers of our Authentic Selves. We must learn to respect them. We must learn to listen," Sarah Ban Breathnach writes in *Simple Abundance*.

This process of identifying projections brought what was running unconsciously in my client into consciousness where he could hear the whispers of his Authentic Self. He was also able to identify, own and accept his projection, stepping out of his unwillingness to own the best within him and into the dream that resides in his heart.

So Marcus' ability to see the best in his friend was really just his friend mirroring back to Marcus the best within himself. My client's opportunity was to own the best within himself and experience himself as the loving being that he is, regardless of what he was going through. Marcus knew exactly what he was doing. He just couldn't see it until he saw it; he didn't know he knew until he knew.

Persian poet Rumi described that place where I work with my clients, "Out beyond ideas of right-doing and wrong-doing, there's a field. I'll meet you there."

As a USM-educated, Soul-Centered Professional Coach, I meet all my clients there—out beyond ideas of right-doing and wrong-doing. And in that place, we learn who and what we truly are. We discover the dreams that reside in our hearts. We learn to own instead of disown our projections, including that part of us that didn't know we knew until we knew. We know exactly what we're doing.

What a blessing,

what a treasured friend

that despair turned out to be.

It continually crushed

my ongoing attempts

at manufacturing optimism,

slowing me down, leveling me

so I could return to love and begin

again and again.

CHAPTER 20

WHATEVER THE QUESTION, LOVE IS THE ANSWER

Sometimes, I am filled with optimism, and sometimes, I am not. This morning, I am not. In the past, I'd have to find a reason. I'd have to blame my lack of optimism on someone or something, demanding that it return lickety-split.

Not now. Now I notice that I'm not filled with optimism, and I love that other part of me, too. I love that other part of me who feels more mellow, maybe a little sad. I no longer demand that I be any different or feel any different than I do right now, in this moment.

It's a little tricky some mornings because the part of me who wants to blame is still there, threatening to take over, making demands, trying to control things. She folds her arms indignantly across her chest, scowls and shakes her head, poking her disapproval at me, sharp and dangerous. I used to be so afraid of this inner drill sergeant that I'd stand at attention and comply with her demands, doing whatever she wanted.

Not now. Now, I see her, I smile, and I turn to that more mellow part of me. I put my arm around that more mellow part of me and tell her it's okay to feel exactly how she feels. I love her, and what that really means is I've learned to love me, all parts of me. Now, I offer myself gentleness instead of cruelty, patience instead of anger, acceptance instead of rejection.

But I wasn't always like that.

It used to be that I was terrified of who I might be if I stopped identifying with my optimism, if I stopped defining myself only as an optimist, complying with that demand inside myself to show up happy. Who would I be without that? Would anybody like me? Would I like me?

I was terrified of finding out that at my core I was some kind of monster, some kind of negative, depressed, horrible being who was utterly miserable. So I let that inner drill sergeant control me, thinking at the time that she was protecting me; maybe she was, but not in the way I imagined.

You'll remember in my story about the Three Musketeers that my forced optimism (a demand of that inner drill sergeant) could not sustain me through all that despair; even though I believed at the time that my optimism could not be extinguished. What I'm aware of now is that the flicker of something else sustained me.

Looking back, my heart goes out to my family, especially my parents, who watched me struggle mightily with that despair. I remember my dad saying, "Lo (my nickname), where are you? I miss you." And my only reply from deep inside the despair was, "Dad, I miss me, too."

And my mom. I don't think I could begin to describe what it was like for her. She came and stayed with me and my girls for over a month during the worst of it. She cooked and cleaned and kept things going. She's really, really good at that. And what a blessing her presence was. She came up with something that needed to be done every day—like replacing the burnt orange tiles that had covered all the floors in my home since 1978, making it look like Mike and Carol Brady and their six kids lived here.

We went together to the hardwood floor store and chose new walnut floors. I don't know if my mom knew what she was doing for me, but watching those dated tiles come out and the new hardwood floors go in gave me hope, offered me the subtle possibility that all may not be lost. Perhaps something new and beautiful would emerge. And it did.

I have the following words written on the wall in my family room: *Whatever the question, love is the answer.*

The question today seems to be this: How can I relate to myself without slipping into despair or falling into the old pattern of manufacturing optimism?

The answer, according to those words on my wall, is love. Be loving. Treat myself as someone I love very much. Perhaps love, not optimism, was that flicker that sustained me in all that despair.

What a blessing, what a treasured friend that despair turned out to be. It continually crushed my ongoing attempts at manufacturing optimism, slowing me down, leveling me so I could return to love and begin again and again. That despair zapped my energy, drained me, so I no longer could make up stories about how I thought the world should work day after day after day. I just couldn't do it anymore. Even my inner drill sergeant's bullying no longer motivated me to tow the line, conform, control, show up happy no matter what. I just didn't have the energy.

Theoretical physicist and philosopher Albert Einstein said, "The significant problems we face cannot be solved at the same level of thinking we were at when we created them."

That soul-shaking despair that seemed like my enemy eventually changed my level of thinking so I could solve the significant problems I thought I had. I didn't see it at the time, but that despair that nearly paralyzed me was caused by my own thinking. It was not caused, as I believed back then, by anyone or anything that was happening outside of me.

I don't look back and blame myself for the thinking that brought that despair. I look back and see that I was doing the best I could at the time. Today, I can meet myself right where I was back then, without judgment, without condemnation, with gratitude for doing the best I could. I didn't know then what I know now. To make myself wrong for not doing better then is demanding against the process, or in other words, thinking that I should have been or could have been different than I was (an old pattern that inner drill sergeant used to motivate me that actually kept me stuck).

I think what really surprised me was the awareness that the despair was not against me. It actually ended up working for me, serving me in the most unexpected ways. Slowly, I learned to adjust my thinking away from despair, away from the misunderstanding that I had done something terribly wrong and deserved to be punished, away from the misunderstanding that what had happened in my marriage was somehow my fault.

That despair led me to a different quality of thought that came from and through love. Slowly, over time, I learned what those words written on my wall meant. My mind became a servant to my heart. My mind became a servant to love. Slowly, over time, I learned to relate to myself from and through love. I learned that whatever the question, love is the answer.

French writer and poet Antoine de Saint-Exupery said it this way, "It is only with the heart that one can see rightly; what is essential is invisible to the eye." It was only through seeing with the eyes of my heart that I could up-level my thinking and come from a place of loving, finding solutions to my perceived problems by allowing new meaning and new interpretations to emerge.

That soul-shaking despair taught me that I could stop buying into the misunderstanding that I caused what happened, that I was somehow to blame, and that I should not/could not ask for help. Despair taught me to stop the debilitating need to appear strong and independent and instead to ask for and receive support, lots and lots of support.

Somehow that despair slowed me down to the speed at which I could let something new in, a new possibility, a new quality of thought, a new way of being inside myself, a new way of understanding how the world worked. Despair opened the door to love and let love in. And letting love in led me to the practice of letting it all be okay. And I mean everything, all of it, letting it all be okay—everything happening inside me as well as outside me.

When I let it all be okay, I reside in a place of neutral observation and learning. I see through soul-centered eyes that what's happening, no matter what it is, is simply earth school curriculum meant for my highest growth and learning. Nothing, nothing, nothing is working against me. It's all for me. Everything, everything, everything is working for me. I am deeply loved, profoundly supported. We all are.

Letting it all be okay is living so fully in the loving that even that inner drill sergeant can take a break, rest and realize she doesn't have to work so hard. If I'd let the drill sergeant have her way with me today, who knows what I would have manufactured to write about this morning. Certainly not this.

She hates vulnerability and can't abide what she judges as weakness. So I gently and benignly ignore her. I don't give her any air time. I smile at her folded arms, her scowling disapproval, her shaking head, her demands, and I go on about my business, writing. I send her love, too, no longer afraid that she is who I really am. I know who I really am, and I serve that part of me now, that part of me who knows herself as love.

When I let it all be okay, I reside in a place

of neutral observation and learning.

I see through soul-centered eyes that what's

happening, no matter what it is, is simply

earth school curriculum meant for my

highest growth and learning.

Nothing, nothing, nothing

is working against me.

It's all for me.

Everything, everything, everything

is working for me.

When we take responsibility

for our own happiness

and stop expecting our partners

to make us happy, relationships improve.

In other words, when we reside

in a place of loving inwardly,

liking everything he does in this case,

then sometimes the quality

of the relationship improves,

and we enjoy being in it more.

CHAPTER 21

IN THE END,
EVERYTHING WILL BE OKAY

I have a sign on my fridge, a magnet that reads: *In the end, everything will be okay. If it's not okay, it's not the end.*

This must be the end of something, perhaps thinking things should have been different than they were, or I should have been different than I was. This must be the end of that because today, everything is okay.

One of my clients has been married to the same man for many, many years. She came to see me right before she and her husband went on vacation, just the two of them, leaving their kids at home. She wanted it to be a good vacation, to really enjoy herself. She wanted both of them to really enjoy themselves.

She's a good woman, married to a good man. They've built a beautiful life over their many years together. But sometimes, he drives her crazy. Sometimes, it's what he does. Sometimes, it's what he doesn't do. She loves him dearly; she isn't going anywhere, neither is he; that was clear to me. So she came to see me to talk about letting it be okay between them, really letting it be okay, so they could really enjoy themselves on this vacation.

As she sat in my office and I felt the purity of her intention, the sincerity of her love, I said (the synergy between us working its magical alchemy), "If you really want to enjoy this vacation, then like everything he does. Everything. Just like it, whatever it is. Don't let anything he does drive you crazy. Let everything be okay."

Shifting slightly in her chair, she said with a touch of concern, "You mean like everything he does, don't let anything drive me crazy, forever?"

"No, not forever! Now that would be crazy!" We both broke into laughter. "Just for the next ten days, while you're on vacation. Don't let anything he does or doesn't do drive you crazy. Just like everything he does while you're on vacation, then see what happens."

"Isn't that sort of going backwards, like a return to the way things were in 1950s? Are you sure about this?" she asked.

"No. I'm not sure about this," I said honestly, "so don't trust this, just try it. Test it. See what happens. Here's the thing … the evolutionary difference between the 1950s and today … you're not liking everything he does to please him. You're liking everything he does to please you, to have what you say you want, which is to really enjoy yourself on this vacation."

"Oh, I see. So what you're saying is to take responsibility for myself, for my own enjoyment on this vacation, simply by liking everything he does."

"Yes. That's it. When we take responsibility for our own happiness and stop expecting our partners to make us happy, relationships improve. In other words, when we reside in a place of loving inwardly, liking everything he does in this case, then sometimes the quality of the relationship improves, and we enjoy being in it more."

"It's worth a try," she said smiling. "My intention is to enjoy this vacation by liking everything my husband does for the next ten days!"

My client really got it. We talked about how what he did or didn't do wouldn't determine whether or not she enjoyed herself on this vacation. What would really make a difference was the place she was coming from inside herself. Liking everything he did became a practice for her of coming from a place of loving, a spiritual practice.

It's what German writer and statesman Johann Wolfgang von Goethe may have meant when he said, "To love someone means to see him as God intended him." And to see another as God intended, we must come from a place of loving inside ourselves, as God intended.

When they returned, she showed me their photos. My favorite was of her doing a headstand on top of a mountain they had climbed together. In the photo, with her husband standing proudly beside her, they're both smiling. She's upside down and he's right-side up. And they're both really enjoying themselves.

It was a moment, captured in a photo, of letting all the years they've shared together be okay. Once we get the hang of it, we can build an entire lifetime on those moments.

I wondered if applying the practice of not letting anything drive me crazy, of coming from an inner place of loving, of letting it all be okay, could inform other areas of life too. So I tested it. I set a clear, positive intention to like whatever I write, to let it all be okay, to like everything that gets written. And choosing to like whatever I write seemed to be the end of something. My writing got easier, more fun.

When I like whatever I write, that part of me that longs

for approval gets it. I smile and the writer within me smiles, like my client and her husband on top of that mountain. Even when my writing feels upside down, I choose to like it. I choose not to let anything I write drive me crazy. I let everything that gets written be okay.

My coach Steve Chandler taught me about the distinction between trusting and testing. It's part of what makes him such a brilliant coach. Here's what he said:

"One of the guiding principles for everything is DON'T TRUST IT ... TEST IT. We overrate TRUST and think it has to be there when it doesn't. It comes later. After you experiment. Most people think they have to trust their new client acquisition system, their new career, their new way of doing something and so on. And because they don't trust it yet, they don't do it. But when we learned to swim or ride a bike, we didn't trust it. We experimented. Trust came later. Now, we jump in the water with total trust. We hop on a bike and ride across town. Total trust. Trust doesn't come *first*, but believing that it does keeps us from all the exciting breakthroughs that are waiting for us every day."

So don't trust me or anything I've written. Test it. Test whatever it is that you want to be okay. And while you're at it, come from a place of loving inside yourself. Test seeing and being the most loving version of yourself, as God intended, because in the end, everything will be okay.

"*To love someone means to see him
as God intended him.*"

JOHANN WOLFGANG VON GOETHE

*To see another as God intended,
we must come from a place of loving
inside ourselves, as God intended.*

Mamaw Yates in 1960,
on the day she married her second husband,
Hunter Yates.

CHAPTER 22

ONLY KINDNESS
MAKES SENSE

My ten-year-old daughter, Hadley, sits across the desk from me doing her homework. She gets easily distracted, but when settled and calm, she works quite well. She whispers to herself as she searches for the words that fit into the squares of her crossword puzzle. I watch her, wondering what she will remember, what will stand out in her memory about her childhood.

I remember my 4th grade teacher, Mrs. Owens. She was young and pretty. Her blond curls bounced when she walked. She would line us up, two by two, then bounce us down the hall to the library. I was mesmerized by those blond bouncing ringlets attached to the top of her head. I always wanted my hair to bounce like hers. That was over 40 years ago. She was probably 30 years old at the time so that would make her nearly 70 now. It's impossible to imagine her at any age other than that year she was my young and pretty teacher.

My elementary school days are vividly etched in my memory. Spring Hill Elementary is where I met my best friend of nearly 40 years. We met when we were ten-year-olds, 5th graders in Mrs. Haslem's class.

My best buddy pal forever (BBPF) is named Blard. That's not her real name, of course, but that's her nickname, the name I've called her since we met. And we've called each other BBPFs since 1975, way before anyone ever texted it.

Blard is kind and calm, smart and pretty. She has long, dark hair and beautiful blue eyes. She and her husband went on their honeymoon to Paris, where I was living at the time. She cut all her hair off while they were there, just like Julia Ormond in the movie *Sabrina*.

What a brave thing to do! Blard arrived in Paris with long hair then returned home without it. Thank goodness she let it grow again. It's such great hair. I think Lebanese artist, poet and writer Kahlil Gibran may have written this just for her, "Forget not that the earth delights to feel your bare feet and the winds long to play with your hair."

One thing Blard isn't is prissy, even with that amazing hair. She grew up as an only child, so that made us like sisters. I loved going to her house where it was always quiet, and she loved coming to mine where it rarely was. And she fit right in. Even around my four siblings, she was never shy. She talked so much that my parents affectionately called her motor mouth. In fact, they still do.

I read somewhere that when going through a divorce, like I did in 2006, there's one person who stays with you through the whole process, from the beginning all the way through to the end. Blard was that person for me. She walked through hell with me. Blard kept me here, anchored to the earth.

She sent me a magnet that I put on my fridge where I would see it every day. On it is a quote by British politician and Nobel

Laureate Winston Churchill, "If you're going through hell, keep going."

Blard kept me going. There were days in 2005, 2006 and even 2007, when I didn't want to keep going. I wanted to be somewhere else, anywhere else, where there was less pain, less despair, less heartache. As it turns out, I got what I wanted. I'm in that place now with Blard still by my side.

When things started falling apart in my marriage, Blard put her protective arm around me, and then kept it around me for all the years it took to get to the other side. She spent countless hours on the phone encouraging, comforting and supporting me.

Occasionally, while in the deepest, darkest parts of the journey, she would look ahead of us, checking to see if there was light at the end of the tunnel, wondering when the end would come into sight. She wanted out of there as much as I did, but she wouldn't leave me. She stayed right with me, her arm firmly anchored around me, making certain I kept going. Always kind. Always calm. Always my smart and pretty blue eyed BBPF.

Blard lives in Cohasset, Massachusetts, a little beach town south of Boston. Since I live by the beach in Southern California, I like to imagine that we're bookends on either side of the country. I rarely see her, but we talk often. I love her, and I feel her love for me, every day.

When I was working my way through all the emotions around the divorce, I remember picturing a gigantic stack of firewood that extended all the way from California to Massachusetts. This enormous pile of logs seemed to be waiting to go onto the fire. I mentioned this to her one day, recognizing the choice I had. "Blard," I said, "it's up to me how I want to use this wood, isn't it? I could burn up these logs with anger or appreciate them for their warmth."

I didn't know which way I would go at the time. In the end, after all those emotions had been extinguished, I went both ways and everywhere in between. I expressed a whole lot of anger and a whole lot of gratitude along the way. And she understood; she met me right where I was every day, never demanding that I be anywhere else.

I learned that the wood burns faster and hotter when I'm expressing anger; and boy, there were plenty of days when there was plenty of that. I also learned that the wood burns slower and steadier when I'm expressing gratitude; and there was plenty of that, too.

I don't know how much of that wood is left now. Since the image came to me as I was going through the divorce, I thought it was related to the divorce. It wasn't. As it turned out, that pile of wood had nothing to do with the divorce whatsoever. The wood and its slow and steady warmth turned out to be a metaphor for the many years of heart-centered friendship I've shared with Blard. It turned out to symbolize the love and the warmth that we carry in our hearts for each other. It's been burning for nearly four decades as I write this.

We may have burned halfway through the enormous pile by now, from California all the way to the town of Lebanon, Kansas. That's the geographic center of the contiguous United States, exactly halfway between California and Massachusetts and exactly halfway between me and Blard. The good news is there's still plenty of wood left, an indicator that we still have many more years of friendship ahead of us, at least four more decades.

Strangely and unexpectedly, looking back on it, I'm glad to have passed through hell. More accurately, I'm glad to have passed through hell with Blard beside me. I'm glad to have known sorrow while experiencing so much of her kindness. The second half of Naomi Shihab Nye's poem "Kindness" makes an intimate kind of sense to me now.

Kindness

Before you know kindness as the deepest thing inside,
you must know sorrow as the other deepest thing.
You must wake up with sorrow.
You must speak to it till your voice
catches the thread of all sorrows
and you see the size of the cloth.
Then it is only kindness that makes sense anymore,
only kindness that ties your shoes
and sends you out into the day to mail letters
and purchase bread,
only kindness that raises its head
from the crowd of the world to say
it is I you have been looking for,
and then goes with you everywhere
like a shadow or a friend.

Yes. As I became well-acquainted with sorrow, Blard's kindness went everywhere with me. As I woke up with sorrow and spoke to it, catching the thread of all sorrow and seeing the size of the cloth, Blard sent me into the day with kindness. When I didn't have the energy to raise my own head, she raised her head from the crowd of the world and looked out for me so that I would know kindness as the deepest thing inside, so that I would know kindness as the only thing that makes any sense. Blard helped me to see the many ways I've been surrounded by kindness my whole life.

I come from kind. Mamaw Yates was kind. That's what we called my dad's mom, my paternal grandmother, Mamaw (rhymes with Gramma) Yates. I've always wondered if she liked that name. She never said one way or the other. She just smiled and seemed to be ready for anything. When she was really happy, which was often, her eyes would twinkle, and she'd say with her southern accent, "Whoopee!"

She was soft, round, lovely. My grandmother was kind. She was profoundly kind, living proof that it's possible to be genuinely and consistently kind.

American writer Henry James said, "Three things in human life are important. The first is to be kind. The second is to be kind. The third is to be kind." My grandmother stopped going to school in the 8th grade so she probably never heard of Henry James. But she knew kind, and she certainly knew what was important.

Not long before she died, from her hospital bed in Charlottesville, Virginia, she said four simple words that brought tears to my eyes. "Lori," she said, "you are kind." I remember my surprise and then the sweetness that surrounded me on the other end of the phone, many miles away from her. My intention from that moment on was to be genuinely and consistently kind, my grandmother's brand of loving, gentle, ongoing kindness.

I remember her hands. My Hadley's hands remind me of Mamaw's hands. I'm surrounded by that same sweetness again as I watch Hadley across from me, pencil in hand, still working on that crossword puzzle. I can see Mamaw's hands holding the receiver to her ear the last time we spoke. I can see them folded neatly in her lap, too, while she sat on the couch at our house, ready for whatever happened and perfectly content if nothing happened at all. She was never in a hurry. She didn't have an opinion very often. She always seemed so patient, so willing to wait and see, so kind.

It's hard to imagine that my grandfather, her first husband, beat her. Impossible really to imagine anyone doing anything of the sort to her, but he did. I never knew him. He died long before I was born.

So I guess my grandmother knew sorrow, too. It's never occurred to me until now because the Mamaw Yates I knew was always so content, so sweet, so kind. Early in her life, she must have caught the thread of all sorrows and seen the size of the cloth. Maybe that's why she was so kind. Knowing sorrow as the other deepest thing, she knew it was only kindness that made any sense.

And she, along with my best buddy Blard, reminds me that we live in a benevolent universe. We are, each one of us, surrounded by kindness, the kind of kindness we can't always see, but we can feel it, especially when we attune to it. It's always there waiting for us. It comes from and through everything, surrounding us with sweetness.

It's what Henry David Thoreau may have been referring to when he wrote, "I believe there is a subtle magnetism in Nature, which, if we unconsciously yield to it, will direct us aright." Yes. That subtle magnetism is kindness, loving kindness. It directs us aright and into our inherently loving nature, and then it goes with us everywhere, like my best friend Blard and Mamaw Yates.

I love the flow of just letting it unfold,

trusting the process,

trusting my own knowing

about where to spend my energy

and my time.

I've written my three pages today,

keeping the commitment

I made with myself.

I don't know what will happen.

I know that I am writing.

And I know that I am happy.

CHAPTER 23

I Don't Know
What Will Happen

An aspen tree sits outside my window, its willowy winter branches bare and so beautiful. The ski runs lay just beyond the aspen. Like white rivers, frozen solid, they cascade with stillness down the mountain.

I'm in Park City, Utah. I have been called here, summoned by something or someone unseen. I have answered the call. The sun feels warm on my skin as I sit inside my room receiving the blessings of its warmth through the window.

I don't know why I am here. I don't know what will happen. I know that I am happy, peacefully positioned like a fat cat, relaxed and drinking in the light of the sun's rays, receiving a fresh flow of energy and inspiration.

In my home that I will build here, the morning sun comes through the window where I write. I write in the sun every morning, three pages every day. I must watch the sun today. Its rising and setting will inform me, telling me where to make my nest here, telling me where my sacred sanctuary is nestled within these Rocky Mountains.

The hotel where I'm staying is located at the main intersection in Park City, exactly where roads converge then diverge going in every direction. I love that this is where I've been guided, at a crossroad in my own life. I will plan my next year here, collaborating with Spirit, co-creating what's next.

Bare and so beautiful, the New Year offers itself to me, igniting my curiosity. This is my best year yet, where I become more of me than ever before, where my highest version of myself steps fearlessly forward into the world, that version of me that I have caught glimpses of in dreams and fleeting moments.

The sun's warmth is what's registering most in this moment. Like that fat cat I mentioned earlier, as a teenager I would curl up in the recess of our big bay window in the home where I grew up. Letting the sun shine her nurturing rays on my young body nestled beneath my mom's hanging baskets of green plants, I remember feeling deep comfort, warmth and rest. I must have a bay window where I can curl up, read, write, retreat from the world and be in the healing light and warmth of the morning sun.

As a child, reading wasn't easy for me, but writing always was. My 6th grade teacher, Mr. Watson, encouraged us to write. We even acted in a play that he wrote. He prepared a part, a personalized part, for every person in our class.

Writing has always interested me. And the work of writing, like grammar and diagramming sentences, was easy for me, even fun. I studied English in college, which was more about reading what other people wrote, but it prepared me. I just didn't know it at the time.

Mythologist Joseph Campbell said, "We must let go of the life we have planned, so as to accept the one that is waiting for us." I didn't know when I left my marriage in 2006, that this writing life would be the one that was waiting for me. Letting go of the life I had planned went against everything I believed. Everything. So it took me a while to work up my courage.

I wrote the following at one of Jennie Linthorst's Life-SPEAKS Tuesday night poetry therapy groups, after reading a poem by Yehoshua November called "How a Place Becomes Holy."

Jennie calls her class "poetry therapy" because it's focused more on the healing that comes through writing than on the quality of what gets written. In my experience over many years of Tuesday nights in her home, whatever gets written from the heart has an unmistakable quality to it.

On the Side of the Road Just Beyond the Gate

"Dad," I ask tentatively, not really wanting to hear the answer to the question I'm about to ask, "what happens if I leave my marriage? What happens to me, my girls, our home, our lives in Palos Verdes?"

We sit alone, my dad and me, on the deck of my parent's summer home in Idaho, overlooking Lake Coeur d'Alene.

I wait, not knowing what he'll say but certain he knows. He knows what will happen next. He's my go-to guy, always has been. He won't leave me hanging.

"Lo," he says, using the nickname he's called me for over 40 years. Leaning forward, shifting slightly in his chair, he looks me in the eye and shocks me with his reply, "I don't know. I don't know what will happen."

I feel the panic rise inside me, like the dinner rolls, rising, unbaked, on the counter, just inside the door.

"Okay," I say, my eyes wide, my voice weak with fear. I force myself to swallow, then say again, "Okay."

One thing I know for sure is that if my dad doesn't know what will happen, no one knows. I feel the weight of this as I stand up and do the only thing I can think to do surrounded by so much uncertainty: I walk. Hard. Uphill.

Feeling the breath in my lungs as my feet make contact over and over again with the pavement, I walk.

It's just me, evergreen trees and black asphalt now. An appreciated mixture of opposites—up/down, soft/hard, shadow/light. Bristly green branches heavy with pine cones grow upward into the blue sky while their ragged roots dig downward into the dark soil.

I walk, filled only with the thought that I don't know what will happen. No one knows, not even my dad.

I see my sneakers through my tears as I turn around, step through the iron gate and start downhill, back towards the house.

Step after step, my feet carry me forward, until I stop suddenly, randomly, on the side of the road just beyond the gate. Knowing what must be done, terrified to do it, I stand perfectly still, tears rolling down my cheeks then dropping off, disappearing into the dark soil.

I cannot cling to any of it any longer. I must let go of it, all of it, every bit, until there's nothing left. Life as it is, as I know it, I must let it all go.

I lay it all down, right there, on the side of the road just beyond the gate, all of it. Then I keep walking.

I'm grateful to my dad for not rescuing me that day on the deck even though I desperately wanted him to at the time. I'm glad now that he told me the truth, letting it all unfold exactly as it did, happy now that he did not know what would happen then.

Many years have passed since that day, but I still nod at that place on the side of the road when I go by it, unnoticed by all, except me. I know what happened there. An ordinary place on the side of the road just beyond the gate made holy by what happened there. An unseen, secret sanctuary of perfect, complete surrender.

———— • ◦ • ————

It's late morning now in Park City, and I watch from the window as the sun moves slowly across the sky. I have four mornings here to spend with the sun, four mornings to do whatever I want. I want to write.

I love the flow of just letting it unfold, trusting the process, trusting my own knowing about where to spend my energy and my time. I've written my three pages today, keeping the commitment I made with myself. I don't know what will happen. I know that I am writing. And I know that I am happy.

Thank you, whoever you are, for calling me here, for guiding me to this crossroads, then directing me into this life that I did not plan, the one that was waiting for me.

There it is, to look back with soft eyes

and see the truth of what is,

receiving the blessing of it,

spiraling upward.

Today, I see how all of it

served the highest good in ways

I could not possibly have imagined

while going through it.

CHAPTER 24

THE UPWARD FLOW OF CONSCIOUSNESS

A black and white magpie makes her way up a blue spruce tree as I watch from inside my Park City hotel room, silently observing from behind the window. She hops from branch to branch, close to the trunk, moving upward in a circular pattern. Just as I'm about to close my notebook, she surprises me, spiraling up the tree. I honor her for showing up briefly this morning and sharing her beauty with me.

Her spiraling reminds me of the ongoing upward flow of consciousness that I myself am experiencing and that also seems to be happening in different places all around the world. I'm certain an example of what I mean will occur to me today since what we focus on tends to expand. That little magpie may have appeared to pique my interest and my awareness so that I would know what to focus on. Even her black and white body reminds me of my own black and white way of thinking that is no longer running in me as it did for many years.

I recognize that the black and white way of seeing the world has its own particular purpose because it has become a point of reference for me now. I know very well what it feels like to move into judgment and out of the sweet upward flow of Spirit. Points of reference matter. We need them to measure our growth.

I once heard a student ask Dr. Ron Hulnick, "How will I know when I have grown spiritually?"

Ron replied, "You'll know because the kinds of things that upset you today will no longer upset you. Six months from now, ask yourself if you're still being upset by the same kinds of things. If you're not, that's an indication that you've grown spiritually."

I made a note in my calendar, exactly six months from that date, to ask myself if in fact I had grown spiritually, if I could see the measure of my growth by using upset and inner peace as my points of reference.

It seems to me that the secret to spiritual growth is an ongoing commitment to learning, growing and healing. And by healing, I mean remembering who we really are, reconnecting with ourselves as divine loving beings, spiritual beings having a human experience.

Writer Anaïs Nin said, "We don't see things as they are. We see things as we are."

As we become more and more aware of the loving beings that we are, we seem to become less prone to upset and more attuned to peace. We no longer allow things out there to upset us. We stop taking things personally. We see that what others say or do has to do with them, not us. We see things as we are and respond accordingly. If we see ourselves as loving and know ourselves as that, then we see through the eyes of love and respond with love. We see that everything is made of love.

This reminds me of something journalist and public commentator Bill Moyers reported that Joseph Campbell said to him, "Preachers err, he told me, by trying to talk people into belief; better they reveal the radiance of their own discovery."

Yes, that's it. When we look through the eyes of love and see the truth of who and what we are, we show up in our radiance. The divine being within, being made of light, shines very bright.

The magpie has flown away, but I'm still sitting in the chair by the window looking out at the view. I don't know what it is about these mountains that I love so much. They lie like gigantic sleeping dogs all around me. I imagine that at any moment they could wake up, stretch their limbs that have been bound to the earth for ages, gather their strength beneath them, and break free from the sleepiness that has kept them docile and still, standing up, rising up, way, way up.

They're like good-natured dogs, these mountains. Like oversized St. Bernards lying perfectly still while we hike, bike and ski all over them. I love to ski. In college, I averaged 30 days a year and some years even more. Maybe that's why I love these mountains. They remind me of the freedom I felt skiing down their backs. I even had a personalized license plate, "SKIINXS" (Ski in excess). And that's exactly what I did.

I fell in love with my ex-husband skiing. He was a very serious student, but I convinced him once to go skiing with me on a weekday. I think it was a Thursday. There were five, maybe six of us, who piled into a car and drove up Little Cottonwood Canyon. We skied at Alta or Snowbird. I can't quite remember which.

My ex could ski. I mean he could really ski. We had so much fun that I let myself fall in love with him. Riding the chair lift between runs, he taught me the words to the song "Oh Come

All Ye Faithful" in French. It was lovely. And all these years later, I still remember those words.

I guess my ex and I did what we came together to do. And today, looking out at the mountains, I feel the blessing of it, all of it (our three daughters such sweet containers of goodness and light, our 17-year marriage, our divorce).

Equanimity. That's the quality I'm experiencing today that seems to want to be cultivated very consciously within me. Wayne Muller, in his book *Legacy of the Heart*, describes it this way:

"Equanimity is the ability to experience the changes in our lives, circumstances, and feelings and still remain calm, centered and unmoved. The image most often used to illustrate the quality of equanimity is that of a mountain. The mountain sits there as the sun shines on it, the rain drenches it, it is covered with snow and struck by lightning. Through it all, through all the changing conditions, the mountain remains unwavering. As we cultivate equanimity within ourselves, we learn to be more like the mountain, finding that place of strength and courage within ourselves that enables us to withstand the slings and arrows of being human without feeling overwhelmed by fear."

I hold everything that happened over the past twenty years as a blessing today, finding that place of strength and courage within myself, feeling grateful and peaceful. Maybe that's an indicator that I've grown spiritually. The same kinds of things that used to upset me no longer do, like the divorce and what led up to it.

French writer Marcel Proust said, "The real voyage of discovery consists not in seeking new landscapes, but in having new eyes." Today, with the help of that magpie and the mountains before me, I'm seeing with new eyes. I'm looking through the eyes of love, and it all appears beautiful.

And there's my example of the upward flow of consciousness. There it is, to look back with soft eyes and see the truth of what is, receiving the blessing of it, spiraling upward. Today, I see how all of it served the highest good in ways I could not possibly have imagined while going through it.

I look out my window on the very slopes we skied many, many times together. And after all the heartbreak, all the anger, all the upset, I send my ex love. I would not be who I am, I would not know myself as I do, without him. Today, I bow gratefully to the view before me, reminding me of the time I fell in love with a man who unknowingly woke me up to the divine being within, joyful and triumphant.

What I'm willing to admit

is that my mind,

as it serves my heart,

becomes a very creative place,

capable of surprising ingenuity

and masterful reframes.

And in this incredibly creative place,

my world works for me,

not against me.

CHAPTER 25

WHO'S WILLING TO ADMIT THEY'RE CRAZY?

Today is the first day of the New Year so I find myself asking myself the same question I ask my clients: *What do I want to create this year?*

My answer comes in the form of an intention: My intention is to write a book that flies on wings of peace, carrying blessings all over the world. This book inspires all who read it to live better by loving better. My words support everyone who reads them in cultivating the qualities they wish to see in the world, living in more joy, more grace, more beauty, more abundance, more love, more peace, more sweetness, more awe, more wonder. That's what I want to create this year.

This year, 2014, is known in the Chinese Zodiac as "The Year of the Horse." I googled that, curious about what it meant. Here's what astrologer Susan Levitt wrote on her website:

———————— • ⬥ • ————————

"The year of the horse is a year of fast victories, unexpected adventure and surprising romance. Energy is high and production is rewarded. Decisive action,

165

not procrastination, brings victory. Magical horse has supernatural powers, is heroic, strong and can even fly. A white celestial cloud horse is sacred to the Chinese goddess Kwan Yin. Her white horse flies through the heavens, bringing peace and blessings."

———— • ⬤ • ————

I love how the benevolent universe responded immediately to me by using many of the same words I just used in my intention. What a beautiful synchronicity that the Chinese Goddess Kwan Yin and her celestial cloud horse fly through the heavens bringing peace and blessings. Maybe they've come to help me create what I said I want to create this year, to support me in my intention.

It makes me smile to imagine that they could and reminds me of the Indians my five-year-old daughter, Hadley, saw fighting in our room at night. After recovering from my initial shock, I imagined those Indians could help me, too.

Here's what happened:

———— • ⬤ • ————

"Mommy," my five-year-old says, looking up at me a bit bashfully with her brown eyes, "at night, I see Indians fighting in our room."

She's slept with me since her dad left last year. All I can do is repeat back to her what she's just said, "Honey, at night you see Indians fighting in our room?"

She nods, her brown curls nodding too, emphasizing her certainty that in fact Indians fight in our room at night.

Could she know that Indians, Tongva Indians to be exact, populated this peninsula long before we did? She's only five, so she couldn't possibly know that. No one would have mentioned that piece of Palos Verdes history to her yet. She sees what she says she sees. I see them, too, as she tells me. Indians, bareskinned and fierce, fight in our room at night.

"Hmmm … ," I say, as prickly fear finds its way to my skin's surface. "Are these Indians real like us or more see-through like ghosts?"

"More like ghosts. I can see through them, but they scare me," she replies without a hint of hesitation.

"Ummm … could you speak to them? Maybe ask them to leave?" I ask, raising my eyebrows just a little.

She considers this seriously for a moment then responds, "Yes. I could speak to them. What should I say?"

"Just ask them to leave, Honey. Tell them they're scaring you," I reply as my courage comes to the surface now. "Just ask them to take their fighting outside."

A month passes, maybe two. She's sitting on a bar stool in the kitchen when she tells me, "Mommy, the Indians don't fight in our room anymore."

I feel my back straighten as I turn to glance at her. She has my full attention although I continue acting unconcerned, casually stirring the taco meat on the stove.

"I spoke to them," she says. "They weren't fighting, they were playing. They told me."

"Good, Sweetheart. You're very brave to speak to the Indians," I say, nodding my head and smiling.

What I don't tell her is that I spoke to the Indians, too. I spoke to the Tongva Chief, to be exact. His four warrior sons stand guard around our home now. Outside, at night, one son in each corner.

———— • ➤ • ————

I don't know if either of these imaginings are true, Kwan Yin and her cloud horse or the Tongva chief and his warrior sons. They're certainly not provable. American writer Nora Ephron said, "Insane people are always sure that they are fine. It is only the sane people who are willing to admit that they are crazy."

What I'm willing to admit is that my mind, as it serves my heart, becomes a very creative place, capable of surprising ingenuity and masterful reframes. And in this incredibly creative place, my world works for me, not against me. What I'm also willing to admit is that I feel a whole lot better picturing those four Tongva warriors standing guard outside my home at night.

What once scared and confused me now surprises and delights me. And that's a much more exhilarating place to live. I'm aware that I might be making this up. I'm also aware that whatever used to scare and confuse me might have been made up, too. I don't know which is true or if it even matters. What I know is that living in surprise and delight is a whole lot more fun than fear and confusion.

And I create, with my thoughts, whatever world I want. When my mind serves my heart, it's serving love, the highest energy available. And that makes it easy, effortless really, to be very creative, to let the upside in.

So I let my resourceful mind create what feels most loving, flying through the heavens, bringing peace and blessings. I reframe those things that scared me into new possibilities that surprise me. And that always moves me out of confusion and into delight. It's just a choice, a way of seeing the world and being in the world that I cultivate now. It's so much more fun than the alternative.

Being sane and willing to admit that I'm crazy, I think I'll go talk to the Chinese goddess Kwan Yin about what I want to create this year while my Indian warriors attend to her cloud horse.

And what a paralyzing

misunderstanding

I've bought into in the past,

believing that things

needed to be done a certain way

or in a certain place

in order to be done right.

Answering the call,

living with intention and on purpose,

that's what matters.

And for me that means writing.

CHAPTER 26

WHERE THE GRASS IS GREENER

Will I trust the dream that resides in my heart to serve through writing? To write every day feels like honoring my word, getting better and better at living with intention, saying what I want and meaning it.

On the movie screen of my mind, I see Julia Cameron, one of my heroes and the author of *The Right to Write*. She's writing while sitting at her black lacquered Chinese desk in New York City. I imagine myself, too, writing what serves others as her writing has served me. Yes, that's the lovely part, the beauty in it, to serve through writing.

What would that look like, I wonder, to serve through writing? A woman rests comfortably in her bed. With my book in her hands, she reads what's written within. Warm beneath the covers, she finds comfort within these pages. My words remind her of her birthright, to live well regardless of her circumstances, to live from a state of deep comfort. She knows this comfort is not complacency. This comfort comes from and through knowing that she is living with intention and on purpose, aligned with the dream that resides in her heart.

I sit every morning in my California king-size bed. Comfortable and warm beneath the covers, I write. One day, I might sit at my black lacquered Chinese desk creating the picture of what I think a writer's life should look like. I have a desk sitting in my living room that looks, I imagine, very much like Julia Cameron's. But for now, I write where I sleep, where I dream, and I let it be okay because I'm writing.

My intention is to write, to reserve my finest energy for the page. And what joy in creating a writing space in my big blue bed. I love the freedom in that. What a paralyzing misunderstanding I've bought into in the past, believing that things needed to be done a certain way or in a certain place in order to be done right. Answering the call, living with intention and on purpose, that's what matters. And for me that means writing.

Julia Cameron lives with intention and on purpose. She answers the call, writing three times a day. First, she writes morning pages, then she feeds her animals, then she writes again and then again later in the day. I love the commitment in that and the freedom.

An interesting combination—commitment and freedom. Julia Cameron is committed to what she loves and that keeps her free. Yet her writing doesn't seem to be about any rigid form of discipline. She writes three times a day because she loves to write. Commitment and Freedom. She lets everything serve her writing, then she lets her writing serve her.

I honor my own intentions more now than I did in earlier decades. Since energy follows thought, I set clear, positive intentions that affirm what I intend to create.

Dr. Mary Hulnick defines intention like this:

———— • ⬤ • ————

"Intention involves clarity of purpose and the willingness to act on it. Clarifying your intention is empowering, for it is through aligning your purpose, choices and actions with the outcomes you wish to experience or manifest that you initiate a powerful alignment with the deeper Essence of who you are. Your thoughts, feeling and behavior line up. You experience the taking of dominion within your own consciousness, resulting in inner and outer cooperation as well as in actions that propel you forward in harmony with your intention."

———— • ⬤ • ————

Today, I trust my intentions to set my course, anchor my commitments and propel me forward.

But I wasn't always like that.

In the past, when someone got mad at me, I would get mad at me. If another person misunderstood me or my intentions, then I would collapse into their misunderstanding, too. Their perception of me or my actions overrode anything I thought, even my most heartfelt intentions.

I was overly concerned about appearing nice and that drove my way of relating to others and to myself. I bought wholeheartedly into the misunderstanding that I was who everyone else thought I was. Everyone else always knew better than I did. I was externally referenced, thinking the truth of who I am resided out there somewhere.

Not anymore. My divorce changed all that, allowing me to

let go of my need to appear nice and focus instead on being kind, to myself first, then allowing that kindness to radiate out to others. Slowly, I began to become internally referenced, and slowly, I began to recover from my need to please other people.

This simple statement really helped: When you talk to yourself, say nice things. It became an extension of what many of us were taught as children: If you don't have anything nice to say then don't say anything at all. I finally took those statements inside myself and applied them for my own good.

So now when I talk to myself, I'm committed to saying nice things, to being kind. And what keeps me free is this: If I don't have anything nice to say about myself then I don't say anything at all. It's so simple, and I've known it all along. It just took me a while to use that information in a way that really made a difference.

Catholic writer and mystic Thomas Merton said, "Life is this simple: We are living in a world that is absolutely transparent and the divine is shining through it all the time. This is not just a nice story or a fable. It is true."

I just love that. I mean I really love it. I dedicate my life to it, to seeing the simplicity and transparency of the divine shining through, to receiving the beauty and the blessing even in, or especially in, the most challenging of circumstances.

Let me give you an example. After we separated, my husband said to me, "If I stay with you, I will always wonder if the grass is greener somewhere else."

I wasn't at all sure what to do with that statement when he said it. The nice thing to do would be to let him go. But then there wouldn't be anybody to please. And like I said, I was very attached to pleasing back then. I wondered about this for a long time, and eventually, I let him go.

I don't know if the grass was greener for him somewhere else, part of me hopes so and part of me doesn't. Perhaps this duality is an illustration of where our divinity meets our humanity. That divine part of me that hopes he found greener grass is unconditionally loving, compassionate and wise. And that part of me that hopes he didn't, well, that's the human part, the vulnerable part that gets angry, feels betrayed, thinks I've been wronged and thinks I need protection.

Perhaps our humanity was designed to assist us in accessing the divine within us, experiencing the divine shining through us, reminding us who and what we truly are.

What I want to tell you is that years after letting him go, I found a little sign in Portland, Oregon. It seemed to set things straight inside me and remind me that when I talk to myself to be kind, to say nice things. It sits in my office now, a daily reminder that the divine shines through everything, and that life is simple, beautiful and full of blessings.

On a black background these white words are written: *The grass is not greener on the other side. It is greener where you water it.*

When we look through
the spiritual consciousness,
the lens of love,
we look through and from
a totally different context.
The conditioned perceptual filters
that have been installed dissolve,
and we awaken even more fully
into the truth of who we are —
divine beings having a human experience.

CHAPTER 27

RESTORING TO ESSENCE

D rs. Ron and Mary Hulnick, in their book *Loyalty to Your Soul: The Heart of Spiritual Psychology,* gave the best definition of healing that I've come across, "Within the context of Spiritual Psychology, we think of healing as restoring to essence."

I've already written about how I love creating visioning boards or collages. I mention it again now because healing always occurs during this process. As pictures and words are brought together in unique and unexpected ways, the messages they have for me call into the light what has been hidden in the shadows. When I create a visioning board, I often get lost in the process while some magical alchemy restores me to essence, to the truth of who and what I am.

I recently did a visioning board in an art class based on Julia Cameron's book *The Artist's Way.* I was asked to include pictures that both animated and repulsed me. I was reluctant to glue onto the page the image of a young, adolescent girl wearing a low-cut shirt.

She herself didn't repulse me, but the low-cut shirt on a 12-year-old did. I covered her not yet fully-developed cleavage with the image of a seagull in flight. I also gave her a crown of candles, a crown of light, that I cut from another magazine to make her, or perhaps me, feel better. I wanted her to know that she was surrounded by light.

After creating the visioning board, we were instructed to ask our images a series of questions then record whatever was coming to us as their response.

Below are those questions and how that 12-year-old responded …

Who are you? "I am the one who grew up before my time, the one who acts as if I know what I'm doing, but I don't really know."

What do you need from me? "I am the one who needs your love, acceptance and compassion."

How are you here to serve me? "I want you to know that it's okay not to know what to do. It's okay not to know. We both wear a crown of light."

I didn't recognize this younger one in myself until a couple weeks later.

Somehow, surrounding that 12-year-old with light, crowning her head with candles and speaking with her, seeing her confusion, her sweetness and her innocence, allowed me to see my own. Instead of blaming myself or anyone else for thinking that I had to or that I should grow up before my time, I surrounded that younger one inside of me with light, placing a crown of candles on my own precious head.

This is my restoring to essence, a sweet remembering of who and what I really am—a loving being, then being that, offering that love, that light, to myself and to that younger version of me.

My daughters are ages 13, 17 and 20 now. They remind me of what those ages look like, sound like and feel like. They, like me, are perfectly imperfect beings, full of light. We all are. No exceptions. And when we start to get this, we begin to heal. We experience our own restoring to essence.

So many of us are tired, looking for a place to rest. We grew up before our time due to our own choices or those of others. We carry weariness and broken hearts. We long to be reminded of all that is beautiful. We see beauty outside ourselves, but we miss the projection, we don't claim that beauty as our own. Our exhaustion has caused us to forget that all is one.

We walk among the beauty and know it not as ourselves. We do great harm to ourselves by keeping ourselves apart from that which would heal us, by not taking responsibility for ourselves. We hear the word responsibility and want to head in the other direction (or at least I do). We're already tired, and that word overwhelms us even more, makes us believe that there's even more work to be done before we can rest.

But responsibility simply means the ability to respond. How do we respond, inside ourselves, to those younger ones?

To respond with love is the radical reframe, the return to essence that we long for. To place a crown of lights on our own heads and rest, take a well deserved break from all that negative self-talk. To see ourselves through the eyes of our own loving. To let it all be okay. To own the darkness and dispel it with the light of our own loving. To heal the error of isolation that blocks us, keeping us separate. To provide a place of rest for ourselves, inside ourselves. To remember the forsaken ones within and bring them home. All those younger versions of us who grew up before their time, offering them unconditional loving, acceptance, compassion and forgiveness.

That crown of light serves as an encouragement to own all the disowned aspects of ourselves, to welcome them home and into the light. How? How do we do that? That would be my question to whomever was writing these words. The answer—we look through a different lens than the one we habitually look through.

There are many different kinds of lenses. We choose another and we reframe what we've held in the past to be true. We acknowledge the human factor in ourselves and immediately replace judgments against ourselves with compassion, recognizing that our humanity was designed to call forward our divinity.

When we look through the spiritual consciousness, the lens of love, we look through and from a totally different context. The conditioned perceptual filters that have been installed dissolve, and we awaken even more fully into the truth of who we are—divine beings having a human experience.

Those younger ones within us are the ones longing for our love, acceptance and compassion. Our refusal to give it to them keeps us forever focused outside ourselves for those very things. We think we need others to reflect love, acceptance and compassion back to us because we so stubbornly refuse to give it to ourselves, being so certain, so convinced, of our own unworthiness.

But, it isn't true. It's like the younger versions of us know this because they lived before we made up the story of our need to be worthy in order to have love, acceptance and compassion for ourselves. So they serve us by calling to us in our dreams, jumping out at us off a magazine page, wanting to heal us of the misunderstanding that we deserve to be weary, worn out and exhausted.

As we care for them, becoming our own good mothers and fathers to those younger ones within, they share their light-hearted loving and unfractured freedom with us. We become one within. We own all those disowned aspects of ourselves. Our inner oneness serves outer oneness in the world because inner reality gets reflected in outer experience.

So as we return to the home of our loving hearts, we bring all those younger ones home, too. And as we become more loving, accepting and compassionate within, the world becomes more loving, accepting and compassionate, too.

To be deeply nurtured is what my body/mind/soul seems to want. And I seem to have some rules about when it's okay to nurture myself instead of just doing it. What I really want is to nurture myself and those around me, to open even more fully and love even more consciously.

What would be the most nurturing thing I could do for myself today? A massage, a cup of tea, a meditation by the fire, an uplifting read, a lit candle, a creative expression, a gentle conversation with a dear friend.

Edna LeShan, television host, counselor, educator and playwright, said, "When we truly care for ourselves, it becomes possible to care far more profoundly about other people. The more alert and sensitive we are to our own needs, the more loving and gracious we can be towards others."

I love that Edna LeShan quote. It's such a gentle approach to responsibility, such a loving reframe about what taking responsibility for ourselves means. And I love the definition of healing as a restoring to essence, a remembering of the Authentic Self, the divine loving being within, a return to love, our own inherently loving nature.

Knowing what healing is makes it possible to heal every day. A healing practice is simply to align with love by saying inwardly or aloud, "I am aligning with love, awakening even more fully into the truth of who I am—a divine being having a human experience." And what a healing blessing it is to align with love and experience ourselves as inherently loving beings. I'm aware, too, of how deeply nurturing that is, like placing a crown of light on our own precious heads.

"When we truly care for ourselves,

it becomes possible to care far more

profoundly about other people.

The more alert and sensitive we are

to our own needs,

the more loving and gracious

we can be towards others."

EDNA LESHAN

"When you reside in beauty inwardly,
you reside in radiant health and
well-being."

DR. MARY HULNICK

———————— • ⬤ • ————————

*Claiming our birthright means
living in beauty inwardly
regardless of our outer circumstances.
It means cultivating
the qualities coded in our hearts.*

CHAPTER 28

BE ANY WORD, EVERY WORD
YOU WISH TO SEE

McCall, my oldest daughter, works in a flower shop in Redondo Beach called Magical Blooms. Last night, while I was sleeping, she brought home two identical bouquets of white blossoms (hydrangeas, roses, lilies and sweet peas), placing one silently on my desk and the other on my night stand, right next to where I was sleeping. They were the first things I saw when I woke up this morning.

It's as if a full choir of angels donated their magnificent wings for those bouquets. Each petal rests peacefully, sending a sphere of white light out from within, reminding me that living well is my birthright regardless of my circumstances.

When I'm not looking directly at the bouquets, I imagine the petals, those little feathery wings, settling in, breathing a deep sigh of relief. Releasing anything no longer needed, they seem certain that they have served, fulfilling the measure of their creation. These bouquets, their final acts of grace before retiring for good.

Mahatma Gandhi, leader of Indian independence who inspired peaceful movements for civil rights and freedom across the globe, said, "Be the change you wish to see in the world." These magical blooms seem to be sending a message meant to support me in being that change. They seem to be encouraging me to be the change I wish to see in the world by cultivating the soul-essence qualities written within my heart.

Like freshly popped popcorn balls, the hydrangeas promote sweetness and serene blossoming. The tender roses surrender softly, opening to the light, holding the spiraling certainty that the light can be trusted. The fragrant lilies expand exponentially, sharing their abundance bursting from within. And the sweet peas, the name itself tells their tale of innocence and childlike wonder.

Sweetness, Serenity, Surrender, Openness, Abundance, Innocence and Wonder—all soul-essence qualities written within every heart waiting to be called out from within and cultivated.

Centered within themselves, each flower invokes its own inner knowing. Blooming individually and collectively, these flowers bring the quiet white light of Spirit into form. As they come into resonance with the great heart of the universe, they bring me into that same resonance.

I'm aware that I am writing. I, like the flowers, center myself within myself, invoke my own inner knowing and bloom silently, fulfilling the measure of my creation. I, too, bring the quiet white light of Spirit into form.

Poet Audre Lorde wrote, "When I dare to be powerful, to use my strength in the service of my vision, then it becomes less and less important whether I am afraid."

I am not afraid this morning. These bouquets and my daughter inspire me to be brave, to be the change I wish to see by cultivating the qualities I wish to be, by being any word, every word I wish to see in the world. Brave is the word that wants to be cultivated today.

So I write, using my strength in the service of my vision as love rises within me, flowing out of me and onto the page. I dare to be powerful while bowing in humble reverence to a magical bouquet silently delivered by the hands of an angel in the middle of the night.

In the words of Kahlil Gibran, Lebanese-American artist, poet and writer, "I wake at dawn with a winged heart and give thanks for another day of loving." His words inspire my own, "I wake at dawn to winged bouquets and give thanks for another way of loving."

That I get to write and that you read what I've written feels like the most intimate of friendships. So intimate that I want to whisper these words to you as you're reading, "Thank you for encouraging me with your willingness to read what I've written. Thank you for your letters telling me of the beauty you see and the love that fills your lives. Beauty and loving long for expression. Thank you for being the change you wish to see by cultivating the qualities you wish to be."

I've seen the light shining from your faces as we claim our birthright and bloom together. So it is you, too, who inspires me to keep writing, to keep being brave, to keep using my strength in the service of my vision.

My vision is a world where we see beauty, where love fills our lives, where we cultivate any word, every word we wish to see in the world, where we embody the soul-essence qualities written within our hearts. I see a world where we softly surrender, like the spiraling rose, opening to the light, revealing our essential centers, that place so easily visible in a fully bloomed flower.

Dr. Mary Hulnick said, "When you reside in beauty inwardly, you reside in radiant health and well-being." Claiming our birthright means living in beauty inwardly regardless of our outer circumstances. It means cultivating the qualities coded in our hearts.

I wonder if these magical blooms could speak, what would they say?

"Be brave. Live well. Bloom. Today. Do not wait until tomorrow. Bring the quiet white light of Spirit into form, blessing all who enter your sphere. Share the same space with others. Like the hydrangeas, roses, lilies and sweet peas, all shapes and sizes bring their own blessing. Dare to be powerful. Dare to use your strengths in the service of your vision. Rest assured that the world is unfolding exactly as it should, that you're unfolding exactly as you should. Live every quality written in your heart: Sweetness, Serenity, Surrender, Openness, Abundance, Innocence, Wonder. Be any word, every word you wish to see. Donate your wings, knowing new blessings will replace that which is given in love."

God spoke today in flowers,
and I, who was waiting on words,
almost missed the conversation.

INGRID GOFF-MAIDOFF

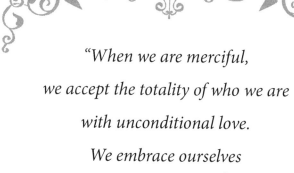

"When we are merciful,

we accept the totality of who we are

with unconditional love.

We embrace ourselves

without judgment, without condition,

and with complete forgiveness.

We see ourselves and others

with soft eyes.

Not with eyes that distort or deny,

but with eyes that attend more gently

to the full spectrum of whatever is true."

WAYNE MULLER

CHAPTER 29

WHAT LOVE FEELS LIKE

M elody Beattie is one of the reasons I write. Reading what she wrote healed me. She's the author of many books: *The Language of Letting Go, The Lessons of Love, Co-Dependent No More, 52 Days of Constant Contact,* just to name a few.

When I'm all by myself, she keeps me company. I gently tucked one of her books into bed with me last night. I couldn't bear to place it away from me, not even eight inches away from me on my nightstand. So I slept with it, tucking it into bed right next to me.

I see Melody's purpose so clearly. She writes from and through her heart. Her writing comes from her life so authentically that it blesses all of us. She writes what's true, no matter what. When reading what she's written, I find myself saying almost audibly to her or maybe to myself, "It's okay, it's really okay."

Another of my favorite writers is Wayne Muller. He wrote the profoundly healing book *Legacy of the Heart.* In it he describes the gift of an unconditionally loving consciousness. Both Melody and Wayne write from and through their unconditionally loving consciousness. Writing from this place inside themselves makes what they write so accessible, so understandable, so healing.

Wayne wrote:

—————— • ⬤ • ——————

"When we are merciful, we accept the totality of who we are with unconditional love. We embrace ourselves without judgment, without condition, and with complete forgiveness. We see ourselves and others with soft eyes. Not with eyes that distort or deny, but with eyes that attend more gently to the full spectrum of whatever is true."

—————— • ⬤ • ——————

Like we did when we were children.

I was shopping yesterday when I saw a tiny pink bunny blanket sitting by the cash register. I think it was meant to be a gift for a newborn baby, a teeny tiny security blanket. I touched it. I couldn't resist. It was soft, so soft and so pink. I wanted it. I wanted to buy it and take it home with me. I really wanted it, but it was a little bit dirty, and I'm a little old for security blankets. So I talked myself out of buying it and left it right there by the register.

But just so we're clear … I wanted it!

I wanted to place it up next to my cheek and run my fingers back and forth across all that double-sided softness. I wanted to feel it up against my skin and melt into the bliss of that pink blanket. It felt like love, or at least it felt like what I imagine love would feel like if I could touch it, hold it in my hands and tuck it into bed with me. There were no rough or sharp edges, only rounded corners and a little bunny face with big ears at the top.

If I weren't the age that I am, I'd carry that bunny blanket everywhere, just to remind me what love feels like. I'd hold it up close to my face and take deep breaths. Not only is it soft, I bet it smells good too. And I'd share it with everybody. I'd let everybody touch it, sharing that fuzzy double-sided softness with them, then they'd understand. I'm sure of it. They'd remember, too, that's what love feels like.

Why didn't I buy myself that blanket? I should have. After all, I am grown up, so I can do whatever I want. Maybe that bunny blanket is still waiting for me to come back and buy it. Maybe it's still waiting right in front of the register wishing that I weren't so grown up, wishing that I'd carried it home with me and let it love me.

I want my friend Melody to have one of those blankets, too. Then it could remind her what she helped me to remember. It could remind her what love feels like, how sweet it is and how it softens all the sharp edges.

We're friends, Melody and me, even though we've never met. Melody is my friend. She writes about her experience of drug addiction and alcoholism, but her books aren't about that. They're about learning, growing and healing. They're about transformation. Melody looks through soft eyes and finds her way to love over and over then writes about what that's like, reminding me.

Psychotherapist Nathaniel Branden said:

"The natural inclination of a child is to take pleasure in the use of the mind no less than of the body. The child's primary business is learning. It is also the primary entertainment. To retain that orientation into adulthood, so that consciousness is not a burden but a joy, is the mark of the successfully developed human being."

———•—◆—•———

I'd love to walk down the street with Melody holding hands and laughing, like girls innocently and naturally do. We could just be playmates and swing our arms back and forth with our hands locked in friendship. We could carry our bunny blankets and they could talk to each other, saying things like, "Hello, how lovely to see you. You're looking quite beautiful today."

We could pretend at being grown ups and giggle at how easy it all seems. We could go back, before addiction, before divorce and before the devastation of losing a child. Melody lost her son Shane, when he was 12 years old, in a skiing accident. It's too much to imagine, too much to understand from where I sit, way too much.

But Melody courageously wrote about it from the same place inside herself where she told me about her addiction and recovery. With the same loving, generous and open heart, she wrote what's true. I'm grateful to her, so grateful to her for sharing her son, her process and her unconditionally loving heart with me.

Melody wrote:

———•—◆—•———

"Gratitude for everything that is in our lives is the key to surrender. And surrender is the key to life. Surrender means we lose control, but it gives us control too. It restores our connection to ourselves, God, life. We become aligned."

———•—◆—•———

What she's written demonstrates how she holds whatever happens to her. It's how she cooperates with what is that makes me want to be friends with her. The inspiration that I feel when I open any one of her books comes from and through her extraordinary consciousness, the unconditionally loving place from which she writes.

I'm not always sure why things go the way they do, but what I am sure of is this: The next time I see a pink bunny blanket, I'm going to surrender and buy it. I'm going to buy it even if it is a little bit dirty. I'm going to love that blanket and let that blanket love me with all its softness, restoring my connection to myself, to God and to life. I'm not so grown up that I've forgotten. I remember the sweetness of surrendering to love, of surrendering to all that softness. I think I'll buy two bunny blankets—one for me and another for my friend Melody Beattie.

The universe is supporting
our awakening into love
every minute of every day
in every one of us.
It's when we come into cooperation
with this evolutionary impulse,
this universal intention,
that what feels like magic
starts to happen.

CHAPTER 30

LA VIE QUOTIDIENNE

Here's what living well is really about. Here's another piece of the code that unlocks the safe that grants us access to the extraordinary treasures contained within our hearts ... Calibrate and align with love, with our own loving hearts, with the Authentic Self, the divine loving being within, every day.

Now if I were reading this, my next question would be, "How? How do I calibrate and align with love every day?"

Jack Canfield, co-creator of the *Chicken Soup for the Soul* series, answered this question when he wrote, "The words 'I am' are the two most powerful words in the language. The subconscious takes any sentence that starts with the words 'I am' and interprets it as a command, a directive to make happen."

Some simple "I am" statements of clear positive intention will calibrate and align us with love every day. Even our subconscious supports us in this process. Here are a few "I am" statements to consider. Feel free to use these or create your own statements of intention.

- I am calibrating and aligning myself with love every day.
- I am living in love.
- I am experiencing myself as a loving being.
- I am aligning with who and what I truly am: Love.
- I am a divine loving being having a human experience.

It's probably easier to make the calibration and align with love if we see through the eyes of the spiritual consciousness, which holds as its foundational tenet that we are divine loving beings having a human experience. From that perspective, we see ourselves through the eyes of love as love, and we begin calibrating immediately.

Cooperating with what is also helps. We cooperate by relating to ourselves as loving beings, as beings worthy of our own loving. We stop making ourselves right or wrong, and we accept our lives and everything that happens as opportunities for growth and learning. We see earth as a school where we each have customized curriculum meant to evolve us. While enrolled in earth school, as we resolve unresolved issues, we move easily into cooperation. In other words, we use whatever happens, even our issues and upsets, to evolve individually and collectively.

These are not my ideas. I heard them first from Drs. Ron and Mary Hulnick at the University of Santa Monica. And the truth is, these ideas were so radical to me at the time that when it actually came to implementing them in my life, I had to hear them over and over in many different contexts in order for them to take root and transform me. That's one of the reasons I wrote this book, to share the many different contexts in which I found that these ideas radically shifted my perspective and profoundly improved my life.

I didn't trust what I was hearing at first. So, as I mentioned earlier, I tested it. I practiced setting clear positive intentions, seeing the loving essence in myself and others and cooperating with what is as best I could. And as I tested these new possibilities, like I said, my life got better, way better.

Mary Hulnick wrote:

―――――――――•――＊――•――――――――

"It's important to know that you need not be concerned about how your intentions will be fulfilled. Our experience is that when your intention is clear, the methods appear. Simply formulate your intentions within the context of *'This or something better for the highest good of all concerned'* and move forward."

―――――――――•――＊――•――――――――

I've also heard Mary say many, many times, "Growth is a process, not an event."

Here's the thing … This process seems to me to be ongoing, even eternal. I see this as a good thing, a blessing, because it supports us in continuing to evolve and in coming into resonance with the evolutionary impulse of awakening into the awareness of ourselves as divine loving beings. I don't know where the end of evolution is. Perhaps it's when we see, experience and know ourselves and each other, as the loving beings that we are, all day, every day. No exceptions.

During earth school, we get to calibrate and recalibrate our energy with love. We get to resolve our issues, many layers of issues, that are designed to bless us, not to frustrate us and certainly not to condemn us or make us feel fundamentally wrong or unworthy. Ultimately, it's our issues and our upsets that assist us in experiencing ourselves as loving beings, coming into cooperation with what is. We get to do these things over and over and over. It's a good thing, really.

My favorite word in French is *quotidienne*. Even the way it sounds as I say it makes me sit up straight and pay attention. When I first heard it, that word got my attention. Having no idea what it meant, I guessed it must mean something very important. Those four syllables just had to be important, attached to sentences spoken by important people doing important things making important decisions.

It means "daily". The word *quotidienne* means daily. It's attached to other words like *le pain quotidien* and *la vie quotidienne* (daily bread and daily life).

At first, I'll admit, I was a bit disappointed. I thought it should mean something more important than that, something more important than daily. And then it hit me ... What we do or how we think or how we live daily *is* important. Very important. Very big and very important.

Why? Because how we live our daily lives (*nos vies quotidiennes*) determines how we live our entire lives (*nos vies entières*). Our days become our weeks, our weeks become our months and our months become our years.

Entier is another one of those grand sounding words in French. It means "whole" and living from wholeness on a daily basis turns out to be somewhat grand and very important.

I remember driving to Santa Monica to turn in my Master's Comprehensive Exam in July 2011. It was a 75-page document in which I had used nearly all 36 USM Basic Skills and 6 Counseling Strategies that I had learned during the two-year program. It was a moment of wholeness in my daily life. I had participated fully, to the best of my ability, and a deep peace settled over me.

I had 20 minutes on the parking meter so after turning in my exam, I sat outside in the meditation garden, closed my eyes and said a prayer of thanks. I had this incredible tingly, alive feeling running through my entire body. I didn't know about the ladder of consciousness yet, but looking back, sitting on that chair in that garden, I was up at the top of that ladder, residing fully in my natural state of well-being, residing fully in my natural state of love.

Just before opening my eyes, just before bringing my awareness back into the world, I heard these words, "This is all there is."

"What?" I asked, quickly trying to capture the source of wherever those words had come from. "What? Wait. What do you mean? What's the 'this' in that sentence?"

Nothing, no response. Whoever said those words seemed to smile then dissipate, leaving me alone with those words in my hands, wondering.

Those words have come back to me in different ways at different times, sometimes with different meanings. What they seemed to mean that day back in July 2011 was this: The feeling of well-being you're experiencing right now is all there is. Daily Wholeness. Everything else is just a story you're making up. This moment of wholeness in your daily life is what's real. Live more fully in these moments of wholeness. The benevolent universe meets you here in a way it cannot meet you anywhere else because this state of well-being is all there is. Calibrate and recalibrate your energy with love because love is all there is. And everything is designed to restore you to wholeness, to love. Everything. Every day.

Once we begin consciously calibrating with love, it becomes much easier over time. Why? Because we stop judging ourselves, and we start seeing how everywhere we've been, everything we've done, where we are now and what we're doing now all serve the process of awakening. Everything, every day, serves the upward flow of consciousness where loving resides, where we reside in our natural state of loving.

I wish this could be delineated into concrete steps, but I don't think it works that way. It feels simpler, softer than that. It feels more like standing still and letting whatever is happening happen, letting the magic happen, allowing it access to us through our stillness.

This upward flow of consciousness is happening in every one of us, regardless of our awareness of it. Which is good news if you think about it. The universe is supporting our awakening into love every minute of every day in every one of us. It's when we come into cooperation with this evolutionary impulse, this universal intention, that what feels like magic starts to happen.

In his revolutionary book *Power vs. Force,* Dr. David R. Hawkins, psychiatrist, consciousness researcher and mystic, describes what this feeling of magic might be:

"The individual human mind is like a computer terminal connected to a giant database. The database is human consciousness itself, of which our own consciousness is merely an individual expression, but with its roots in the common consciousness of all mankind. This database is the realm of genius; because to be human is to participate in the database, everyone by virtue of his birth has access to genius."

———————•—◗◖—•———————

Here's another possibility when looking through the lens of the spiritual consciousness:

———————•—◗◖—•———————

The individual human heart is like a computer terminal connected to the great heart of the universe. The great unconditionally loving heart of the universe is human consciousness itself, of which our own consciousness is merely an individual expression, but with its roots in the common consciousness of all mankind. The great heart of the universe is the realm of loving; because to be human is to participate in the evolution of consciousness, everyone by virtue of his birth has access to loving.

———————•—◗◖—•———————

Calibrate. Recalibrate. Align. Cooperate. Evolve. Daily. This is all there is.

When awareness comes,

it seems to require

a willingness to be still,

let it settle and see what happens.

If I am willing to be still and let it settle,

then what's important and elusive

lets the light shine on it for just a minute.

And in the light, awareness expands,

or more accurately, awareness expands me.

CHAPTER 31

Hot Summer Nights in Virginia

I've written about this already, but it's so important and so elusive that it bears repeating. Both authors Byron Katie and Steven Dahl wrote, "True forgiveness is realizing there's nothing to forgive."

I see this in an obvious way sometimes, like I see what's around me when the sun is shining. At other times, I completely lose sight of it, like at night when there is no moon and even the shapes of things around me are dark, impossible to identify.

When awareness comes, it seems to require a willingness to be still, let it settle and see what happens. If I am willing to be still and let it settle, then what's important and elusive lets the light shine on it for just a minute. And in the light, awareness expands, or more accurately, awareness expands me.

But if I try to catch it, grab it with my hands, hold it hostage and take it home with me, the lights go out. And awareness disappears, dissipates, becomes impossible to identify.

Like fireflies or lightening bugs.

On hot summer nights in Virginia, I would sit with my

Granddad Robey, my mom's dad, on the front steps of his home while thousands of fireflies would light up the darkness around us. Sitting side by side, he would smoke a Camel cigarette while I perched my right elbow on his left knee. Together, we would watch the light show in the forest across the street.

A few courageous fireflies would come into his yard and light up right in front of us. Those were the ones I would catch, grab with my hands, hold hostage, put in a jar and take home with me.

But the world didn't work the way I thought it did.

The ones I caught then put in a jar with holes in the lid so they could breathe were often dead by the next day. And after that first night when I tried to make them mine, if they weren't dead, they wouldn't fly anymore. They would just crawl around the bottom of the jar, over the grass and sticks I'd placed there to make them feel at home.

And they wouldn't light up anymore either.

I didn't imprison all the fireflies I caught. I remember just holding some of them in my hand. If I held one loosely enough, it would light up, transforming my six-year-old hand into a little Chinese lantern, just for a second. Sometimes, instead of putting it in a jar, I would open my hand, let it crawl to the edge of my finger and fly away again. I would follow the light of that one firefly as long as I could, taking it in my hand over and over again, without ever placing it in the jar.

It's been a long time since I chased fireflies.

As I remember those hot summer nights, I feel my love for my Granddad and appreciate the patient way he sat next to me on the steps, watching me as I ran around the yard. He didn't chase fireflies. He just quietly smoked his cigarette while he watched me and the light show going on around me.

He didn't stop me from putting my firefly hostages into a jar. He smiled and helped me poke holes in the lid. He seemed to know, given how I thought the world worked, I was doing my best, holding those fireflies hostage, wanting them to be my friends, to sit by my bed, keeping me company during the night. He let me be exactly who I was, meeting me right where I was at age six, seven and eight. He calmly let me learn what those fireflies were designed to teach me.

My writing coach, Dr. Stellasue Lee, studies the *Tao te Ching* every morning with her husband. As I finished reading this chapter to her this morning, she shared with me what they'd read earlier today. "Purity and stillness are the ideal for the world," she said. "We have to learn not to hold onto things too tightly. We have to learn to let what is just be without forcing it to be anything but exactly what it is." Her wisdom often takes my breath away. I think she may have been talking about more than just fireflies.

The French have an expression: "*Tout comprendre, c'est tout pardonner.*" It means to understand all is to forgive all. I think it's another way of saying that true forgiveness is realizing there's nothing to forgive.

Because it's elusive, I find myself asking, "Can that possibly be true? Can there really be nothing to forgive?"

In those moments when awareness comes, I see that it's possible when looking through the light-filled lens of love. It's then that I become aware that each one of us is doing the best we can, given how we think the world works. Really letting in the possibility that we are all doing the only thing we can do, based on how we think the world works, allows us to see the bigger picture. And once we see the bigger picture, it's hard to return to a narrower view.

Everything, every behavior, makes sense in some context. Once we understand the context, once we compassionately consider the contextual reality of another, then we stop judging and begin noticing. That's when we see there's nothing to forgive.

American poet and writer Henry Wadsworth Longfellow said, "If we could read the secret history of our enemies, we should find in each man's life sorrow and suffering enough to disarm all hostility."

We can extend this way of relating to others, as well as to ourselves, because sometimes we're our own worst enemy. When we look back on our own lives, if we sit still long enough and look through the light filled lens of love, we'll remember how we thought the world worked. Our own contextual reality, at any given time, returns to us. Then we begin to understand our own choices and possibly even see that there's nothing to forgive in ourselves. We too were doing the best we could in every moment. We may even find in our own lives sorrow and suffering enough to disarm all hostility, even towards ourselves.

As kids, we effortlessly embody purity and even a certain kind of stillness. It's easy to see through the lens of love when we're young because we're not always judging ourselves and everyone else. We practice true forgiveness without even being aware that we're practicing or forgiving. Then somewhere along the way, we forget who we really are, and we start imagining the world works differently than it does.

On the cover of this book is a photo I took of my daughter Madison in 2002, when she was six years old. The path on which she walks, illuminated with golden light, seems to have been waiting for her. Even the trees on either side stand at attention as this precious divine being having a six-year-old experience walks among them.

She embodies such purity and stillness at that age, sweetness and love, too. With her arms raised in innocent joy, I can almost see the "clouds of glory" trailing behind her that English Romantic poet William Wordsworth wrote about:

Our birth is but a sleep and a forgetting:
The Soul that rises with us, our life's Star,
Hath had elsewhere its setting,
And cometh from afar:

Not in entire forgetfulness,
And not in utter nakedness,
But trailing clouds of glory do we come
From God, who is our home.

It's 2014 now, and Madison turned eighteen this year. She'll go off to college in the fall with those qualities still very much alive in her, still "trailing clouds of glory." I guess letting her go is my chance to practice learning not to hold onto things (or daughters) too tightly.

Purity and Stillness. Sweetness and Love. We cultivate each of these qualities as we walk the path of our own lives by thinking over and over the kinds of thoughts we wish to dominate our lives, like Thoreau said. Our own purity, stillness, sweetness, love and even preciousness, never leave us. We simply lose sight of them.

Perhaps the light filled path and the trees standing at attention on either side of my Madison are meant to remind us that each one of us embodies those qualities, that each one of us, at every age, is always a precious divine being having a human experience. And perhaps, the path and the trees never lose sight of the "clouds of glory" that trail behind us.

It's been over 40 years since I sat on the steps with my Granddad. What I'm aware of today is this: I captured those fireflies not because I wanted to harm them. I captured those fireflies because I wanted to care for them, take them home with me and love them. I thought putting them in a jar would allow me to do that. That's how I thought the world worked back then.

What it took me many years to learn and what those fireflies may have been designed to teach me is this: Love, like awareness, requires a willingness to be still, let it settle and see what happens. If I am willing to be still and let it settle, then what's important and elusive lets the light shine on it for just a minute. And in the light love expands, or more accurately, love expands me.

Granddad Robey in 1978

We can choose

what we want to cultivate

or let what wants to be cultivated

choose us.

It's a simple process:

Just smile, breathe and

trust what resonates.

CHAPTER 32

THE CODE THAT
UNLOCKS THE SAFE

I used to be a big believer in lists. Not anymore. Today, I prefer a gentler, more organic unfolding. Having said that, a list of sorts seems to want to be included here. Perhaps the code written within these pages wants to be easily accessible, contained in one place.

Theologian and philosopher St. Augustine said 21 centuries ago, "Free curiosity is of more value than harsh discipline."

With that in mind, let's agree to explore this list with humor and grace, with free curiosity. Let's give ourselves and each other the dignity of our process by taking our time, allowing these things to integrate slowly, over time. Let's promise to be gentle, loving and patient with ourselves and each other as these things get drawn out from within us. Let's agree to be as creative as we like, with the intention of using this list to deepen in the awareness of ourselves as divine beings having a human experience.

The following statements can be used one at a time or combined into an infinite number of possibilities. We can choose what we want to cultivate or let what wants to be cultivated choose us. It's a simple process: Just smile, breathe and trust what resonates.

So here it is, the code contained within each one of these chapters. This is the code that unlocks the steel safe I saw sitting in the sand in my dream at the beginning of this book, the code that grants us access to the sanctuary of our loving hearts.

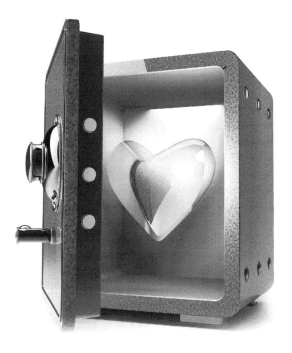

INTRODUCTION • LOOKING THROUGH THE EYES OF LOVE

- Cultivate a consciousness of loving.
- Begin again, every day.
- Experience the gorgeousness of your own unconditionally loving consciousness.

1 • WRITE WHAT'S WRITTEN WITHIN

- Pay attention.
- Warmly express what's in your heart.
- To live well, love well.
- Answer the call.
- Harness the energies of love.

2 • WHAT IF I'M THE ONLY ONE?

- Trust what resonates.
- Go beyond the borders of perceived limitations.
- Contribute. Serve. Inspire.
- Love unconditionally.

3 • THE SHOULDERS ON WHICH WE STAND

- Love deeply that which was not meant to be perfect.

4 • A WARREN BUFFETT-SIZED BANK ACCOUNT

- "The world was made to be free in." – David Whyte

5 • LIFE: A SACRED JOURNEY

- Cooperate with what is.
- Live peacefully in the home of your heart.

6 • **WHAT THE WORLD NEEDS**
  - Follow what you love.
  - Do what makes you come alive.
  - Live full of your own aliveness.

7 • **BUTTERFLIES ARE FREE TO FLY**
  - Smile and breathe.

8 • **BECOMING PART OF PEACE**
  - Honor the light, love, truth, beauty and peace within you.
  - Find your peace.

9 • **TRUE FORGIVENESS**
  - Relate to the divine being in everyone.
  - Practice true forgiveness.
  - Dissolve all barriers you've built against love.

10 • **LET THE BIG HORSE RUN**
  - Release the extraordinary coded within.
  - Live the life you were built for.

11 • **OUR MOST PRECIOUS RESOURCE**
  - Slow down to the speed of life.
  - Practice the wisdom of underdoing it.
  - See the beauty that is all around you and in you.

12 • THE LIGHT SHINES ON AND THROUGH EVERYTHING
- Claim every version of yourself.
- "Put down the weight of your aloneness."
  – David Whyte
- "Ease into the conversation." – David Whyte

13 • REFRAMING ISSUES AS BLESSINGS
- Remember, FEAR is Forgetting Everything is All Right.
- Let everything work for you, not against you.
- Create any future you dare to imagine.

14 • COMING HOME
- Remember, anything is possible.
- Update, up-level, rebuild, transform.
- Claim your own beauty, worth and value.

15 • D'ARTAGNAN AND THE THREE MUSKETEERS
- Don't Decide Before.

16 • LETTING THE UPSIDE IN
- See the upside.
- Contain life and all its duality.
- Attune to and align with love.
- Be open, gentle, expansive.

17 • SAVING MS. TRAVERS
- Be the creative owner of your own destiny.
- Live in your natural state of being which is well-being.

18 • GOD'S MASTERPIECES
- Discover the dream that lives in your heart.
- Pay attention to your inner vision.
- Create the world as you wish it to be.
- Live as God's masterpiece, as a center of pure loving awareness.

19 • I DIDN'T KNOW I KNEW
- Own the best within you.

20 • WHATEVER THE QUESTION, LOVE IS THE ANSWER
- Meet yourself right where you are.
- Let it all be okay.
- Remember, you are deeply loved, profoundly supported.

21 • IN THE END, EVERYTHING WILL BE OKAY
- Come from a place of loving inside yourself.
- Don't trust it. Test it.

22 • ONLY KINDNESS MAKES SENSE
- Be genuinely and consistently kind.
- Let kindness direct you aright and into your inherently loving nature.

23 • I DON'T KNOW WHAT WILL HAPPEN
- Step fearlessly forward into the best version of yourself.
- Surrender completely to love.

24 • **Seeing Through the Eyes of Love**
  - Remember, everything is made of love.
  - "Reveal the radiance of your own discovery."
    – Joseph Campbell
  - Consciously cultivate equanimity.
  - "Like a mountain, remain calm, centered and
    unwavering." – Wayne Muller
  - "Find that place of strength and courage
    within yourself." – Wayne Muller

25 • **Who's Willing to Admit They're Crazy?**
  - Create with your thoughts whatever world you want.
  - Live in love, the highest energy available.

26 • **Where the Grass is Greener**
  - Align with the dream that resides in your heart.
  - Live with intention and on purpose.
  - When you talk to yourself, be kind, say nice things.
  - See the divine shining through everything.
  - Where you want the grass to be greener, water it.

27 • **Restoring to Essence**
  - Heal by being restored to the essence of
    who you truly are.
  - Know yourself as an inherently loving being.
  - Respond with love.
  - Place a crown of light on your own precious head.

28 • **Be Any Word, Every Word You Wish to See**
  - Cultivate the qualities written within your heart.
  - Be brave. Live well. Bloom. Today.

29 • WHAT LOVE FEELS LIKE
- Look with the soft eyes of the heart.
- Be grateful.
- Surrender and restore your connection to love.

30 • LA VIE QUOTIDIENNE
- Let yourself be restored to wholeness.
- Remember, love is all there is.
- Access your genius and your loving.
- Calibrate. Recalibrate. Align. Cooperate. Evolve. Daily.

31 • HOT SUMMER NIGHTS IN VIRGINIA
- Be still, let things settle and see what happens.
- Remember, every behavior makes sense in some context.
- Be compassionate and disarm hostility.
- Look through the light-filled lens of love.

32 • THE CODE THAT UNLOCKS THE SAFE
- Explore with humor, grace and free curiosity.
- Be gentle, loving and patient with yourself and others.
- Take what is most meaningful to you and use it.
- Look for more of the code in your daily life.
- Keep practicing.
- Cultivate the divinity coded within.

33 • INSIDE THE SANCTUARY OF OUR UNLOCKED HEARTS

- Remember, you are are an elegantly designed divine being currently enrolled in earth school.
- Participate in the real work going on in the world— evolution in consciousness.
- Relax and remember, perfection is in the process and in the plan, not in you.
- "Let the soft animal of your body love what it loves." – Mary Oliver
- Offer yourself love, acceptance, compassion and forgiveness.
- Live in the sanctuary of your unlocked heart.
- Release the unlimited supply of extraordinary treasures coded within you.

There may be more of the code that you're seeing in these pages that I'm not seeing. I hope so. Please take from this book whatever is most meaningful to you and use it. And continue to look for more of the code in your everyday life. It's everywhere if we have the eyes to see it. I've included a couple of blank pages at the end so you can write whatever occurs to you, so you can record the code that you've discovered, the one that grants you access to your own loving heart.

And remember, we promised to be gentle, loving and patient with ourselves and each other. We promised to allow these things to get drawn out from within slowly, over time. This is a natural, organic process that's not meant to be completed all at once.

Here's why … This code, every part and particle of this code, is already written within each one of us. These things don't come in from the outside. They're drawn out from within, naturally and organically, over time, as we become aware of them, as we awaken, when we're ready.

As we return to the sanctuary of our loving hearts again and again, we are restored to the truth of who we are over and over. And as we become more and more aware of the truth of who we are, we get better and better at releasing the extraordinary coded within.

And here's another part of the code (maybe the most important part): We get to keep practicing. Like learning to play an instrument or a sport or to speak a foreign language, we get to keep practicing, and eventually over time, mastery results. Eventually, we find ourselves residing in love, attuned to and aligned with all that is. We find that we, more often than not, are thinking the kinds of thoughts we wish to dominate our lives. And with those thoughts, we are gracefully and easily cultivating the divinity coded within us.

As we return to the sanctuary

of our loving hearts

again and again,

we are restored

to the truth of who we are

over and over.

And as we become more and more

aware of the truth of who we are,

we get better and better

at releasing the extraordinary

coded within.

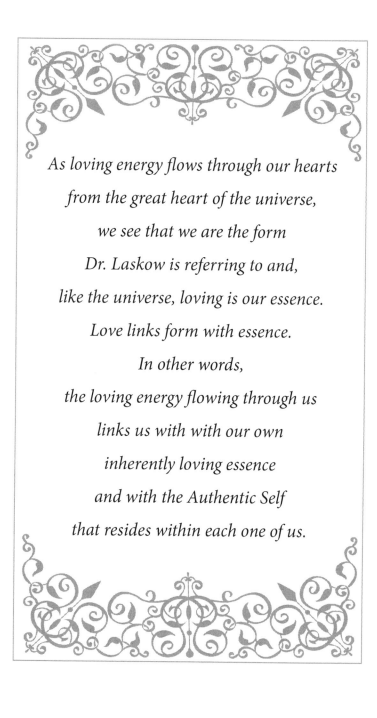

As loving energy flows through our hearts

from the great heart of the universe,

we see that we are the form

Dr. Laskow is referring to and,

like the universe, loving is our essence.

Love links form with essence.

In other words,

the loving energy flowing through us

links us with with our own

inherently loving essence

and with the Authentic Self

that resides within each one of us.

CHAPTER 33

INSIDE THE SANCTUARY OF OUR UNLOCKED HEARTS

I heard Dr. Mary Hulnick say recently, "The most conscious woman I know still has unresolved issues." This came as quite a relief to me because it means more of the code has yet to be revealed, even to the most evolved among us. As long as we're here, enrolled in earth school, most of us will have ongoing issues to resolve.

Again, in the words of Mary Hulnick, "You are a Divine Being with an Earth School curriculum designed perfectly to support you in Awakening into the Majesty of the Love that you are." This evolution in consciousness is the real work going on in the world. And it takes the time that it takes. There's no hurry.

As we learn to resonate with love, aligning with our own unconditionally loving hearts, we're not meant to live perfectly. There's no perfection in the way we go about unlocking our hearts and releasing the extraordinary coded within. We do this perfectly imperfectly over many, many years. The perfection is in the process and in the plan, not in us.

We don't have to be anything other than ourselves in order to do this work of awakening. So there's nothing to worry about. We're just encouraged to live well by loving well. And when we find ourselves out of balance or out of alignment, we can gently and with great love remember: It's all part of the plan.

"Wild Geese," written by the Pulitzer Prize winning poet Mary Oliver, is such a beautiful illustration of this. Mary Oliver so elegantly reminds us that when we move out of balance and into despair or upset, the world supports us in returning to balance by "offering itself to our imagination, announcing our place in the family of things."

Wild Geese
You do not have to be good.
You do not have to walk on your knees for a
hundred miles
through the desert repenting.
You only have to let the soft animal of your body
love what it loves.
Tell me about despair, yours, and I will tell you mine.
Meanwhile the world goes on.
Meanwhile the sun and the clear pebbles of the rain
are moving across the landscapes,
over the prairies and the deep trees,
the mountains and the rivers.
Meanwhile the wild geese, high in the clean blue air,
are heading home again.
Whoever you are,
no matter how lonely,
the world offers itself to your imagination,

calls to you like the wild geese,
harsh and exciting, over and over announcing
your place
in the family of things.

from *Dream Work* by Mary Oliver
published by Atlantic Monthly Press
© Mary Oliver

Going out of balance assists us in seeing what's seeking resolution so we can resolve it and bring ourselves back into balance. It also supports us in seeing that the benevolent universe offers itself to us, surrounding, protecting, enfolding and encouraging us with love.

I've heard Dr. Ron Hulnick say many, many times, "When any one of us resolves an issue, the whole human family evolves." We participate in that evolution every time we bring ourselves back into balance, back into alignment with our natural state of loving, simply by letting the "soft animal of our body love what it loves." We gently return to love, the truth of who we are in the deepest sense, by offering ourselves love, acceptance, compassion and forgiveness.

Poet and writer Kahlil Gibran said, "Tenderness and kindness are not signs of weakness and despair but manifestations of strength and resolution." I know. It sounds too good to be true. Too simple. Yet when we are tender and kind inside ourselves, offering ourselves love, acceptance, compassion and forgiveness, our divinity embraces our humanity and oneness results. We are no longer divided inside ourselves or against each other.

Dr. Leonard Laskow is a Stanford-trained physician who has studied the healing power of love over the past four decades. I attended one of his workshops a couple of years ago and was profoundly touched by the loving and heartfelt way he shared his many years of research and learning with me.

In his book *Healing With Love*, he writes, "Love, at its deepest level, is the awakening to Oneness. When loving presence flows through the heart, it shifts the vibration of the inner energy body into resonance with our essential nature— with the truth of who we really are and with the truth of what is. It is love that links form with essence."

As loving energy flows through our hearts from the great heart of the universe, we see that we are the form Dr. Laskow is referring to and, like the universe, loving is our essence. Love links form with essence. In other words, the loving energy flowing through us links us with with our own inherently loving essence and with the Authentic Self that resides within each one of us.

As we awaken to oneness, inside the sanctuary of our unlocked hearts, we find an unlimited supply of extraordinary treasures coded within us waiting to be released:

———— • ◆ • ————

Abundance, Acceptance, Alignment, Aliveness, Attunement, Authenticity, Awareness, Awe, Balance, Beauty, Benevolence, Calm, Clarity, Coherence, Compassion, Confidence, Cooperation, Courage, Creativity, Direct Knowing, Empathy, Enthusiasm, Equality, Equanimity, Forgiveness, Freedom, Generosity, Gentleness, Genuineness, Giving, Grace, Gratitude,

Goodness, Goodwill, Happiness, Harmony, Healing, Honesty, Humor, Imagination, Innocence, Inspiration, Integrity, Intuition, Joy, Kindness, Light, Loving, Loyalty, Luminosity, Majesty, Mercy, Nurturance, Openness, Patience, Peace, Preciousness, Presence, Radiance, Receptivity, Relaxation, Resonance, Respect, Reverence, Self-Expression, Serenity, Service, Silence, Simplicity, Softness, Stillness, Strength of Heart, Support, Surrender, Sweetness, Tenderness, Tranquility, Unconditional Loving, Vitality, Warmth, Willingness, Wisdom, Wise Counsel and Wonder.

———•—◆—•———

Any and every one of these treasures, these soul-essence qualities, when consciously cultivated, is enough to radically transform our inner worlds bringing us into oneness and into resonance with our Authentic Selves. And as we experience this transformation inwardly, we revolutionize our outer world as well.

Perhaps poet and philosopher Henry David Thoreau said it best, "What lies before us and what lies behind us are small matters compared to what lies within us. And when we bring what is within out into the world, miracles happen."

From inside the sanctuary of our unlocked hearts, attuned to and aligned with the truth of who we are, we see ourselves as we are. We are the miracle that love brought into form. We are the presence of love. We are elegantly designed beings currently enrolled in earth school, extraordinarily gorgeous creations made from, through, in and of love. Every one of us. No exceptions.

"The miracle is not to walk on water.
The miracle is to walk on the green earth,
dwelling deeply in the present moment
and feeling truly alive."

THICH NHAT HANH

Consciousness Is Its Own Reward

This book seems to want to begin and end with a dream. Just last night, I had another dream … I'm a new resident in a small town where all the townspeople have gathered together to celebrate. What they're celebrating isn't quite clear to me, but they're all very kind and include me in the festivities.

Someone in the crowd announces that an older member of the community is going to get her hair cut. Everyone cheers then moves in unison to the hair salon to continue the celebration there. I think this is a bit strange, so I ask the person next to me, "What's going on? Why are we celebrating and what's so important about this particular woman getting her hair cut?"

"Nothing," is the reply. "We're not celebrating anything in particular, and there's absolutely nothing at all important about this woman getting her haircut. It's the start of summer, and the tradition in this town is that everyone accompanies this woman to get her hair cut every year. No one knows when this tradition started or why, we just look forward to seeing each other and celebrating."

When I'm not judging this tradition as strange, it's just fun. So in the dream, I go along with everyone else, getting caught up in all that ordinary joy. Nothing particularly fabulous or even interesting is happening. We're just all together, having fun and celebrating.

When we get to the salon, the older woman sits in the chair and gets her hair cut. And we keep doing exactly what we were doing at the other location and all along the way—animatedly talking, laughing and really enjoying ourselves, happy about wherever it is we're headed.

Like those five beings that were walking on the water in my first dream, this second dream embodies a similar kind of energy. Only this time, no one is walking on water. We're just walking on an ordinary street in an ordinary town on an ordinary summer day, celebrating.

Vietnamese Zen Buddhist monk Thich Nhat Hanh said, "The miracle is not to walk on water. The miracle is to walk on the green earth, dwelling deeply in the present moment and feeling truly alive."

Consciousness. The highest of human capacities—an unconditionally loving consciousness. That's the miracle. And the reward. Yet residing in a consciousness of loving isn't about the miracle or the reward. Residing in an unconditionally loving consciousness is the miracle and the reward. It is, in and of itself, miraculous and rewarding.

An unconditionally loving consciousness is that state of being that accepts what is, loves what is, and stops the compulsive outward search for acceptance and approval. It's an inner reality, an inner quality of being. And it aligns us with who and what we truly are: Love.

It becomes our inner reality when we consciously cultivate

it. Our hearts open to love, every kind of loving, and we become aware that we are souls whose essential nature is love. We are all there is in that moment. We are the presence of love. Love is present because we are present. We are love.

Perhaps this is enlightenment. And perhaps it's also the miracle we're really after—the experience of walking on the green earth, animatedly talking, laughing and really enjoying ourselves, happy about wherever it is we're headed, dwelling deeply in the present moment, feeling truly alive, knowing ourselves as love.

When I imagine residing in an unconditionally loving consciousness, here's what occurs to me ... I'm standing in front of big industrial-strength doors as they slide slowly open, and I have a new experience of something very ordinary. Behind the doors, I see something or someone I've judged harshly in the past as beautiful in the present. And all the judgment I once felt just dissolves inside me. And I'm at peace.

Then, later, I come to another set of big industrial-looking doors. As they slide wide open, I see a situation that I've judged in the past as terrible transform into something lovely, and again I'm left in gratitude and peace. This second experience is no different than the first. In fact, it feels almost identical. Yet these opportunities to experience myself as an unconditionally loving consciousness seem to be building on each other.

Perhaps true enlightenment is sliding open that final door, slowly pulling or pushing those heavy metal doors wide open, one more time. Only this time, we forget about judging entirely, and we just love whatever's before us. We become one with whatever's happening behind those doors. We don't judge any of it anymore so there are no more doors to open. Nothing needs to be hidden any longer. We have access to everything because we're not judging any of it. We just go along for the ride after that, seeing the beauty in all of it, celebrating.

And we no longer expect there to be a reward, nor do we need a reward, because experiencing the gorgeousness of our own unconditionally loving consciousness is the best reward there is. Nothing tops that moment when we come into alignment with our own Authentic Selves and know ourselves as we truly are—as souls having a human experience, as the presence of love. And we see everyone as we see ourselves. We don't need anything after that. It's like we got what we came for.

The Elders of the Hopi Nation declared in a prophesy in August 2000, "All that we do now must be done in a sacred manner and in celebration. We are the ones we've been waiting for."

Maybe the first experience of consciousness is absolutely no different than the last. What's different, what sets the first apart from the last, is where we're coming from inside ourselves. Consciousness has built on itself. And eventually, when that last door opens, we live "in a sacred manner and in celebration" because we see that we are the love we've been seeking.

And we see that there was no need to have hurried through any of it. There's no hurry. And there's nothing to worry about either.

The more willing we are to meet ourselves right where we are along the way, the easier it all becomes, the more grace-filled and peaceful. The grace and peace are always there, every step of the way, we just become more and more aware of them as we become more and more aware of ourselves as loving beings, as we walk through all those doors.

In the end, everything is okay, not because it's any different than it's ever been, but because we're seeing it differently, through different eyes, through a lens that's become more and more aware of where to focus and what to focus on.

So on an ordinary day, in an ordinary town, we focus on love and get caught up in all that ordinary joy as we accompany an older woman to get her haircut. We become part of what is and the miracle happens. We awaken more fully into the awareness of ourselves as divine loving beings immersed in a human experience. Joseph Campbell said it this way, "The privilege of a lifetime is being who you are."

Consciousness of ourselves as we are is the real miracle.

Consciousness of ourselves as we are is its own reward.

As we awaken and stand forward in the radiance and glory of who we are, as we look through the eyes of love, we see for ourselves what the Hopi Elders saw, "We are the ones we've been waiting for."

Dear Reader,

The following questions for reflection and discussion are optional. I've included them at the end of this book for those who would like to further explore what's written within these pages. I invite you to explore first the questions that correspond with the chapters that resonate most within you. Trust what resonates. And trust your own knowing on how to best use these questions.

Would you prefer to answer them on your own in a notebook where you discover for yourself where your mind, your heart and your hand might take you? Or would you prefer to discuss them with a friend or with a group of friends where you can discover together what's coded within your hearts? There's no right way or wrong way of doing this, just settle in and attune to the gentle voice of your heart.

If you've received what you needed from this book simply by reading what's written within it, then there's no reason to answer any of these questions. My heartfelt encouragement is to test trusting your own wisdom. You know better than anyone else what's best for you. Honor that.

"My soul honors your soul. I honor that place in you where the entire universe resides. I honor the light, love, truth, beauty and peace within you because it is also within me. In sharing these things, we are united, we are the same, we are one." Namaste.

QUESTIONS FOR REFLECTION AND DISCUSSION

INTRODUCTION:
LOOKING THROUGH THE EYES OF LOVE

If you knew that you were an extraordinarily gorgeous creation made from, through, in and of love, how would you relate to yourself today? In what ways would you care for and nurture the extraordinarily gorgeous creation that you are?

In what ways are you willing to cultivate looking through the eyes of love? List a minimum of three ideas that occur to you as ways of cultivating your own loving essence.

On a scale of 1-10 (10 being fully aware), how aware are you of yourself as a loving, creative, peaceful, joyful, beautiful and compassionate soul having a human experience? In what ways could you support yourself in becoming more aware?

In what ways can you practice seeing the loving essence in yourself and others today? How willing are you to be compassionate and loving, no matter what's happening, with yourself and with others?

Throughout the day, in what ways do you align yourself again and again with love, creating a continuous feedback loop to the truth of who you are, connecting you to your natural state of being? How could you support yourself even more in fully aligning yourself with love?

1 · WRITE WHAT'S WRITTEN WITHIN

My mentor Mary Hulnick once asked me, "If there were a sacred dream that has been held in your heart from the time that you were little, a vision that you've held for yourself in this life … what would it be?"

Do you have a sacred dream or vision that you've held for yourself in this lifetime? If so, what would it be?

Who would you be and what life would you be living if you answered the call of your deepest dreams and moved into the world that mythologist Joseph Campbell called "original experience," where you could decide for yourself what matters and what doesn't?

Teilhard de Chardin discovered the fire of love that burns in every heart when he wrote, "You are not a human being in search of a spiritual experience. You are a spiritual being immersed in a human experience."

In what ways does your inner world shift and your view of the outer world transform when you consider the possibility that you are a spiritual being immersed in a human experience?

2 · WHAT IF I'M THE ONLY ONE?

Persian poet Rumi said, "Let yourself be silently drawn by the strange pull of what you love. It will not lead you astray."

In what ways are you allowing yourself to be silently drawn by the strange pull of what you love? In what ways are you resisting that pull?

How do you respond to the voice within that casts doubts on your inner intelligence and wisdom? How do you respond to your inner intelligence and wisdom when it asks, "What if I'm the only one?"

For me, the Endeavor became a symbol of grace. She brought a way of loving without condition to this human experience. Who or what do you use as a symbol to inspire you and remind you of the mastery that's possible?

3 · The Shoulders On Which We Stand

If you were to name your home, like my friends Lisa Bay and Sean, what name would you give it? Why?

Who are the people who have influenced your life who are no longer here? In what ways do you stand on their shoulders? How have their words and lives made you a better person?

If something old must die for something new to be born, how can you honor that which must die or has died, recognizing the gifts and blessings of what came before?

President Reagan said, "It always seemed to me that JFK was a man of the most interesting contradictions, very American contradictions … One sensed that he loved mankind as it was, in spite of itself, and he had little patience with those who should perfect what was not meant to be perfect."

In what ways do you demand that you or those around you "perfect what was not meant to be perfect"? Are you willing to love yourself and all mankind as it is, in spite of itself? In what ways do you or those around you demonstrate this quality of genuine kindness?

Is there a hand written note you could write thanking someone in your life for their eloquent and graceful leadership, perhaps someone on whose shoulders you now stand?

4 · A WARREN BUFFETT-SIZED BANK ACCOUNT

Has your heart ever been "shattered day after day, like a carefully handblown Italian crystal water goblet intentionally dropped on a hard, cold marble floor, repeatedly?" How did you respond? Did those sparkling shards of your broken heart turn out to serve you? How?

Could it be that it is only through feeling profoundly alone that we can find our heart's ultimate connection to all things? How has aloneness served you?

In David Whyte's poem "Sweet Darkness," he writes, "You must learn one thing." What would you write on the blank page beneath that line? In other words, what's the one thing your soul longs to teach you?

5 · LIFE: A SACRED JOURNEY

The following is one of the best definitions of peace I've come across: "Peace. It does not mean to be in a place where there is no noise, trouble or hard work. It means to be in the midst of those things and still be calm in your heart." (author unknown)

What is your definition of peace?

What's the distinction between desperately attempting to control things in order to establish some level of comfort and accepting what is from a place of grateful acknowledgment and gentle rejoicing?

What does your home reflect about you? Like my friend Colleen, is your home a place of peaceful contentedness, an outer reflection of your inner beauty? If so, what do you like best about your home? If not, what small changes could you make that would enhance the peacefulness of your surroundings?

Why do you think that people with big challenges, like cancer, often slow down and treat life as more sacred and precious? Are you willing to slow down without a big challenge and experience the kind of peace that loving brings?

6 · What the World Needs

Preacher Howard Thurman said, "Ask not what the world needs. Ask what makes you come alive … then go do it. Because what the world needs is people who have come alive."

What makes you come alive? What's your jumping off point, your edge? What exhilarates and excites you, even scares you?

Are you ready to break through the fear of who you tell yourself you are, and instead, meet your most courageous self, that part of you who wants to know what's possible?

What inspires you to risk what could be? What keeps you from risking?

Is there a radical risk you're currently taking or wanting to take? If so, what?

Are you willing to live full of your own aliveness, like Shane McConkey? List three ways you could live more fully in your own aliveness.

7 · BUTTERFLIES ARE FREE TO FLY

Like the blue butterfly that I glued into my notebook, is there an image that you could use to support you in your transformation? What might that image be?

Susan Jeffers wrote, "Every time you encounter something that forces you to handle it, your self-esteem is raised considerably." What could you handle today that would raise your self-esteem considerably?

What's your favorite song? Could the lyrics have a message for you that might assist you in your transformation?

Is there a new beginning being disguised as a painful ending occurring in your life? In what ways are you willing to ask for and receive Spirit's assistance?

What can you do today that would allow you to let go of what others think and begin caring for yourself with loving and compassion?

8 · BECOMING PART OF PEACE

Hemingway wrote, "If you are lucky enough to have lived in Paris as a young man, then wherever you go for the rest of your life, it stays with you, for Paris is a moveable feast."

Whether or not you've lived in Paris, in what ways do you experience your life as "a moveable feast"?

If you knew that everything in the physical world was a metaphor for something deeply spiritual, what metaphors occur to you? What might these outer metaphors be reflecting to you about your inner reality?

Elizabeth Gilbert wrote in her book, *Eat, Pray, Love,* "We

don't realize that somewhere within us all, there does exist a supreme self who is eternally at peace."

Do you have access to that part of you who is eternally at peace? If so, how do you access that part of yourself? If not, what could you do to support yourself in having an experience of that eternally peaceful part of you?

The awareness of ourselves as containers of peace spans many centuries. The following examples provide evidence of this awareness—the 21st century American writer Elizabeth Gilbert, the 19th century English writer Martin Fraquhar Tupper, the 17th century translation of the King James Version of the Bible, the 14th and 15th century German monk Thomas à Kempis, and the Namaste greeting that dates back to 3000 BC to 2000 BC.

What other evidence of ourselves as containers of peace are you aware of?

If peace were the global and universal icon of humanity and everyone everywhere recognized it, how would you show up differently in your world today?

Imagine a world where everyone became part of peace like Gertrude Stein became part of the view in Kent's painting. Could it be that the real peace we are seeking already exists? Could it be that peace is just waiting for us to become part of it?

9 · TRUE FORGIVENESS

Ask yourself what Neale Donald Walsch asked at the end of his speech in Los Angeles, "Are there any assumptions you're holding that you would be willing to question and have your own conversation with God?"

Steve Dahl wrote, "If you saw the illusions for what they really are, you'd recognize you have never been slighted or harmed. You'd recognize there was never anything to forgive. True forgiveness is recognizing there is nothing to forgive."

How can you apply true forgiveness in your life? Where do you feel slighted or harmed? Can you see any other possibilities? Is it possible that whatever happened is serving you, encouraging you to learn and grow? If so, how?

What are you ashamed to tell someone you admire? What do you not want others to know about you? Is there someone in your life with whom you'd be willing to share your secrets? If so, whom?

If you knew that sharing what feels most vulnerable would serve your awakening, what would you be willing to share?

Are there any barriers you've built within yourself against love? If so, how can you dissolve those barriers and return to your true nature, your natural state of loving?

10 · LET THE BIG HORSE RUN

Dr. Jean Houston said, "We all have the extraordinary coded within us waiting to be released."

What are the fearful thoughts that might be stopping you from getting into gear and releasing the extraordinary coded within you?

How can you use fear as your ally, turning it to your advantage by remembering what FEAR really is: Forgetting Everything is All Right?

Is there someone you could ask for assistance? A friend, a mentor, a coach? What's stopping you from "placing yourself in the slipstream" of someone "older, steadier and more experienced"?

Race cars and thoroughbred horses are metaphors that inspire me. What are some metaphors that inspire you? How can you use those metaphors to awaken that part of yourself that wants to experience what it's like to get in gear, see what you can do, live the life you were built for?

11 · OUR MOST PRECIOUS RESOURCE

When we slow down, sometimes way down, that's when we rise up and see the beauty that is all around us, the beauty that is always around us. And if we slow down even more, then we start to see the beauty that's in us, the preciousness, worth and value that was there all along.

What do you imagine the negative consequences would be of slowing down? What might be the upside of slowing down? In what ways would you be willing to slow down if you knew that slowing down was a return to knowing yourself as your most precious resource?

Many poems are found within the pages of this book (see Poems in the index for titles, authors and page numbers). Which one resonates most within you? Would you be willing to use the poem that most resonates as a jumping off point into your own creative self-expression? What form of self-expression would be the most fun for you? Writing? Painting? Poetry? Dance?

Chinese writer Lin Yutang said, "Besides the noble art of getting things done, there is a nobler art of leaving things undone."

What are you willing to leave undone today in service to slowing down and experiencing your own beauty, preciousness, worth and value?

12 · THE LIGHT SHINES ON AND THROUGH EVERYTHING

Like the light in our Point Vicente Lighthouse, if there were a 1000-watt light bulb inside your chest rotating at exact intervals, what would you want it to shine on and what would you prefer it didn't disturb? Where would you want the windows of your inner world to be painted black to provide you with some privacy?

Are you willing to become, as David Whyte writes, "unutterably yourself," accepting all parts of yourself at all ages, even the most difficult, the least perfect? In what ways can you see the perfection in the seemingly imperfect? In yourself? In others?

David Whyte also writes, "Put down your aloneness and ease into the conversation." He then talks about the kettle singing to you and the cooking pots seeing the good in you. What in your world wants to be in conversation with you? What is it that encourages you to eradicate the "great mistake" of believing you are alone? What in your life enables and encourages you to experience that "everything is waiting for you"?

If you knew that "everything is waiting for you," what action would you take today? What conversation would you have?

13 · REFRAMING ISSUES AS BLESSINGS

Often, underneath anger is fear or hurt. Do you ever get angry? What fear or hurt might lie beneath the surface of that anger? Do you have a persistent question that's seeking resolution, a fear that comes out as anger? If so, what?

How do you relate to yourself when you experience feelings of inadequacy, anger or concern? Do you quit, blaming yourself or others, and move into despair? Or are you able to reframe those thoughts and feelings, allowing them to work for you instead of against you, offering yourself compassion and even forgiveness?

Video game designer Jane McGonigal defines an Epic Win as "an outcome so extraordinarily positive that you had no idea it was even possible until you achieved it. It's almost beyond the threshold of imagination and when you get there, you're shocked to discover you're capable of it."

In your current reality, what would an Epic Win be for you?

Are there issues in your life that you might be willing to reframe as blessings, discovering the opportunity inherent in whatever is happening, allowing those issues to work for you instead of against you? What would an example of this be in your own life?

14 · COMING HOME

If you were to write, filling one line after another, snaking your way in straight lines from left to right, back and forth across the page, where might your mind, your heart and your hand take you ? Like Henry Miller, are you willing to write to find out what you're writing about? Or sing to find out what you're singing about? Or dance to find out what you're dancing about? Or paint? Or draw? Or laugh?

Writing is my way of making a deep mental path, thinking over and over again the kinds of thoughts I wish to dominate my life. Writing is my way of supporting myself in letting the upside in.

What is your way of supporting yourself in letting the upside in, in thinking the kinds of thoughts you wish to dominate your life?

If you knew for certain that we create reality with our thoughts, what kind of thoughts would you choose to dominate your life?

As I sat on my couch in Paris and followed the flowing designs of my wrought iron balconies, they became a blueprint for my writing. What blueprints for your life have been imprinted inside of you?

Ramanuja, 11th century Hindu theologian and philosopher, said, "What we seek as our highest goal depends upon what we believe ourselves to be."

Who or what do you believe yourself to be? Are you willing to see new possibilities and update outdated assumptions and beliefs about yourself with something new, something more beautiful?

If you were to imagine yourself as a house, like C.S. Lewis talked about, and you received a loan to completely refurbish and reconstruct it, where would you begin?

15 · D'Artagnan and the Three Musketeers

What do you consider your best quality? Have you ever lost sight of it, or like me, not been able to find even a flicker of it inside you? What happened? Did that quality return or did it get replaced by something else?

In what ways are you pretending to know what will happen or demanding that you should know what will happen before it happens? In what ways are you bullying yourself into some form of compliance to your inner demands because you're afraid of the vulnerability inherent in not knowing what will happen?

Are you willing to consider living by the motto the Three Musketeers brought me: Don't Decide Before? What does Don't Decide Before mean to you?

If the Three Musketeers were to show up in your dream with a motto for you, what might that motto be?

16 · Letting the Upside In

Is there a situation in your life that could assist you in looking for the upside, in recognizing the positive, favorable or advantageous aspect, in finding opportunities for growth and healing?

The lyrics of the song "Little Wing" by Sting supported me in my awakening. Is there a song, a poem, or a quote that might support you in yours?

Do you, at times, buy into the misunderstanding that you have *to do* something in order *to be* lovable? Are you willing to consider the possibility that you're lovable regardless of anything you do or don't do?

For years, I lived inside of my own crushing judgment and demand for perfection. No one did that to me, except me. I was my own worst enemy. In what ways are you your own worst enemy? What are some ways you could become your own good company?

If you knew that the cosmos was made of love and that you are a way for the cosmos to know itself, in what ways would you be willing to allow love to flow through you? In what ways would you be willing to let the upside in by attuning to and aligning with love?

17 · SAVING MS. TRAVERS

Is there anything in your life that's happened that you're still thinking should not have happened, keeping you in a victim position at the bottom of the ladder of consciousness? If so, what?

Where are you on the ladder when you bring this memory back and give it new life? Are you willing to reframe what's happened, looking through a different lens than the one you habitually look through, finding the opportunities and blessings in any challenging situation, allowing your life to work *for* you instead of *against* you?

Walt Disney said it this way, "Aren't you tired of remembering it that way? Don't you want to finish the story and have a life that isn't dictated by the past?"

And my coach Steve Chandler said it this way, "Life is like a movie with many endings. Give me any situation in your life, anything, and I'll ask you one question: Given what you just told me, what would you like to create?"

Consider any situation that's happening in your life right now, anything. Now ask yourself Steve's question, "Given what's happening, what would you like to create?"

In what ways can you use self-acceptance, self-compassion and self-forgiveness to move yourself up the ladder? Are you willing to come into peace with the past, collecting the gifts and blessings of whatever the past holds in service to living well now?

18 · God's Masterpieces

Have you ever created a visioning board or collage? If you were to create "a kind of story board or blueprint of the life you want to create, a wish map," what kinds of images would you glue onto the page?

Are you willing to set aside any fear you might be feeling and allow the dream that lives in your heart to be translated into the world of three dimensions through visioning? Are you ready to let your curiosity about what might get created carry you through to the other side?

I encourage you to create a visioning board then ask what you're creating as it's coming into form, *What do you need from me? How can I serve you?* Then give it what it needs. Let it share with you how you can serve it.

And once that visioning board has come into form, then ask, *Who are you? What message do you have to share with me?* Now, let the visioning board answer. Write both the questions and answers on a piece of paper and glue them to the back of your board.

Imagine, as God's masterpiece, that the universe wants to give you what you need, to serve you. If the universe were to ask you these questions, how would you answer them, *What do you need from me? How can I serve you? Who are you? What message do you have for me today?*

After experiencing Mary Hulnick's guided meditation, in what ways do you experience yourself as a center of pure loving awareness?

If you knew that you were God's masterpiece and allowed your very being to be a free flow of love, what world would you create for yourself?

19 · I Didn't Know I Knew Until I Knew

Willa Cather wrote, "She heard a deeper vibration, a kind of echo, of all that the writer said, and did not say."

In your inner world, while listening with the ears of your heart, can you hear a deeper vibration inside of you that knows exactly what you're doing?

If you knew that you know exactly what you're doing, how might you show up differently in your world today?

I invite you to explore the same questions I ask my clients: *What is it you want? Why do you want this? What's the goal beneath the goal or what's the inner experience you're really after? Deep down, at the purest level of knowing, what is it you really want to create?*

Now explore this question: *Who do you admire and why?* Write down some of the qualities you admire in whomever comes to mind.

Now review the qualities you just wrote down. (I gently remind you that you could not see these qualities in the person you admire if they didn't already exist in you. You simply would not/could not see them.)

Drs. Ron and Mary Hulnick wrote, "The disowning of the best within us allows us to maintain unworthiness, dependency, helplessness, and of course, anger associated with disempowering ourselves."

Are you willing to own the qualities you wrote down about the person you admire? Are you willing to own the best within you and see yourself as the divine loving being that you are? In what ways could you support yourself in this process, in owning instead of disowning the best within you?

20 · WHATEVER THE QUESTION, LOVE IS THE ANSWER

Is there an inner drill sergeant inside of you that folds her arms indignantly across her chest, scowls and shakes her head, poking her disapproval at you? Do you comply with her demands? Or are you able to accept all parts of yourself even those parts that the drill sergeant says are unacceptable, those parts that feel more mellow, maybe a little sad?

When you consider the phrase, "Whatever the question, love is the answer," what does it mean to you?

Can you think of a time when experiencing the depths of despair actually served you and led you back to clarity?

Do you look back at your life with love or do you blame yourself and demand that you could have or should have done better than you did? Are there situations in your life where you could apply loving to your own experience and see that you were doing the best you could? How might you meet yourself right where you were at any given time, without judgment, without condemnation, with gratitude for having done the best you could?

If you knew that what has happened or what's happening now, no matter what it is, was simply earth school curriculum meant for your highest good, how could you use what's happening for your most profound growth and learning?

List three examples from your life that indicate everything is working for you.

21 · IN THE END, EVERYTHING WILL BE OKAY

What's stopping you from having what you say you want? What haven't you been willing to let be okay that would allow you to take responsibility for your own happiness?

In what ways are you expecting someone else to make you happy?

How could coming from a different place inside yourself facilitate change as well as a happier experience of being you?

If you knew that in the end, everything will be okay, how would you show up differently in your world today?

Johann Wolfgang von Goethe said, "To love someone means to see him as God intended him."

What might support you in coming from a place of loving inside yourself, allowing you to see those you love as God intended? How could you come from a place of loving and look with the eyes of love today?

To what other areas of your life can you apply the practice of coming from an inner place of loving, of not letting anything drive you crazy, of letting it all be okay?

My coach Steve Chandler taught me about the distinction between trusting and testing. What part of your life are you still trying to trust? What might happen if you tested it instead?

22 · ONLY KINDNESS MAKES SENSE

What do you remember from your childhood? What memories stand out in your memory about your life? Are you aware of any kindness that surrounded you? If so, what?

Like me, has there ever been a time in your life when you felt like you were going through hell? What kept you going? What or who kept you here when you wanted to be somewhere else, anywhere else, where there was less pain, less despair, less heartache?

Have you had experiences that allowed you to "catch the thread of all sorrows" and "see the size of the cloth"? Once you saw the size of the cloth, how did you integrate into your own heart Naomi Shihab Nye's awareness "then it is only kindness that makes sense anymore"?

If you knew that only kindness made sense, how would you show up differently in your world today?

Are you aware of how the benevolent universe is trying to make itself known to you by the subtle kindnesses you experience every day? In what ways are you being surrounded by kindness now?

23 · I Don't Know What Will Happen

What version of your most radiant self have you caught glimpses of in dreams and fleeting moments? What life does that version of you inspire you to create?

Mythologist Joseph Campbell said, "We must let go of the life we have planned, so as to accept the one that is waiting for us."

If you knew that the life waiting for you is better than anything you could have planned, what would you be willing to let go of?

After reading "On the Side of the Road Just Beyond the Gate" on pages 155-157, what do you have to say about how a place becomes holy? Where might your unseen, sacred sanctuary of perfect, complete surrender be?

24 · Seeing Through the Eyes of Love

Anaïs Nin said, "We don't see things as they are. We see things as we are."

When you look through the eyes of love and reconnect with yourself as a divine loving being, how does the outer world reflect back to you your inner experience?

Have you ever been able to grow past some of your old resentments and heartbreaks and find a new context in which to put them? If so, how did that new context change your life?

How do you track your spiritual growth? If you knew that spiritual growth could be tracked by marking a date in your calendar six months from today, then asking yourself on that date if the same kinds of things that upset you six months ago are still upsetting you today, would you do it?

If you knew that life was serving your highest growth and learning and that everything that happens was customized curriculum meant to restore you to a place of strength and courage within yourself, would it make it easier or harder to see yourself through the eyes of love? Why?

25 · Who's Willing to Admit They're Crazy?

If the Chinese Goddess Kwan Yin and her celestial cloud horse could fly through the heavens bringing peace and blessings, what would you ask them to help you create this year?

Nora Ephron said, "Insane people are always sure that they are fine. It is only the sane people who are willing to admit that they are crazy."

What's the difference between being crazy and the *fear of looking crazy?* If you never had any fear of looking crazy, how would your life be different?

If it's true that you create with your thoughts whatever world you want, what world would you like to create? What things scare you that you could reframe into new possibilities that surprise and delight you?

When your mind serves your heart, it's serving love, the highest energy available. In what ways can you support your mind in becoming a servant to your heart?

26 · Where the Grass Is Greener

What does answering the call or living with intention and on purpose mean for you? How does living with intention and honoring your intentions set you free? In what ways do you honor and respect your own intentions and commitments?

In your mind, what's the difference between being nice and being kind? Why does it matter that you focus on being kind to yourself first, and then allow that kindness to radiate out to others?

Are you ready to apply the wisdom you've heard since childhood, "If you don't have anything nice to say then don't say anything at all," inside yourself and apply it in a way that really makes a difference? In other words, when you talk to yourself, are you willing to say nice things or nothing at all? Can you see the usefulness of talking to yourself with kindness?

Catholic writer Thomas Merton said, "We are living in a world that is absolutely transparent and the divine is shining through it all the time." Share three examples of where you experience the divine shining through your world.

In what ways are you aware of where your divinity meets your humanity? How has your humanity—that part of you that feels vulnerable, gets angry, feels betrayed, thinks you've been wronged and thinks you need protection—assisted you in accessing the divine within you where unconditional loving, compassion and wisdom reside?

Where is the grass greenest in your life? Are you watering what you want to cultivate or are you imagining that the grass might be greener somewhere else?

27 · RESTORING TO ESSENCE

In their book *Loyalty to Your Soul: The Heart of Spiritual Psychology,* Drs. Ron and Mary Hulnick wrote, "Within the context of Spiritual Psychology, we think of healing as restoring to essence."

What does that phrase "restoring to essence" mean to you? In other words, what is the truth of who you are on a spiritual level? What do you think your essence is?

I encourage you, like my instructor Helen Bradley encouraged me, to look through magazines and tear out images that both animate and repulse you. Then create a collage with those images. Are there any images you would like to surround with light, like that image in my collage of the 12-year-old in a low-cut shirt?

Once your collage is complete, ask the images the following questions and record the answers that come to you: *Who are you? What do you need from me or how can I serve you? How are you here to serve me?*

Are you aware of any ways that the process of creating this collage has restored you to essence? What was your experience throughout this process? Did you experience a sweet remembering of yourself as a loving being, a perfectly imperfect being, full of light?

If you knew that you were a loving being, full of light, how would you treat yourself? How would you speak to yourself? How would you be with yourself?

Are you willing to remember those forsaken ones within and bring them home? If you were to look through the lens of love, how would you offer the younger versions of yourself love, acceptance and compassion? What would you say to them? How would you be with them?

What would be the most nurturing thing you could do for yourself today? What's something you could offer yourself that would be the equivalent of placing a crown of light on your own precious head?

28. BE ANY WORD, EVERY WORD YOU WISH TO SEE

What does it mean to you when you read the words, "Living well is our birthright regardless of our circumstances?"

Spiritual and political leader Mahatma Gandhi said, "Be the change you wish to see in the world."

What change do you wish to see in the world? What inner qualities could you cultivate that would support you in being that change? List a minimum of three qualities that you would like to cultivate.

Today, how could you be brave? What's the vision you see for the world? What strengths do you have that you could use in service to your vision?

When my daughter brought me those white bouquets, it felt like a full choir of angels, complete with wings, had landed in my room. Have you ever received a gift that inspired you? If that gift could speak, what message might it have for you?

Please send me an email or write me a letter telling me about the beauty you see and about the love that fills your life. (www.loricashrichards.com).

29. WHAT LOVE FEELS LIKE

Who inspires you? Is there anyone whose work inspired you so much that it gave your life direction and purpose like Melody Beattie's writing did for me?

Wayne Muller wrote, "When we are merciful, we accept the totality of who we are with unconditional love. We embrace ourselves without judgment, without condition, and with complete forgiveness. We see ourselves and others with soft eyes. Not with eyes that distort or deny, but with eyes that attend more gently to the full spectrum of whatever is true."

What does it mean to you to see yourself and others with soft eyes? What does it mean to attend more gently to the full spectrum of whatever is true?

Melody Beatty wrote, "Gratitude for everything that is in our lives is the key to surrender. And surrender is the key to life. Surrender means we lose control, but it gives us control too. It restores our connection to ourselves, God, life. We become aligned."

Are you grateful for everything that happens in your life? The seemingly good as well as the seemingly bad? How willing to surrender to all that happens are you? How aligned are you, with yourself, with God, with life?

In what ways could you surrender completely to the power of love? Do you remember what love feels like? What might you use to remind you?

30 · La Vie Quotidienne

Writer Jack Canfield wrote, "The words 'I am' are the two most powerful words in the language. The subconscious takes any sentence that starts with the words 'I am' and interprets it as a command, a directive to make happen."

What "I am" statements would you like your subconscious to interpret as a command, a directive to make happen? Create a minimum of three "I am" statements.

In what ways do you align daily with love? How are you currently relating to yourself as a divine loving being, worthy of your own loving? In what ways could you support yourself in living more fully into this awareness?

Do you have a favorite word in English or in another language that gets your attention like the words *quotidienne* and *entier* got mine? Google your words and see what they mean. Explore how your words might support you in living more fully.

If you knew that David Hawkins got it exactly right when he said, "Everyone by virtue of his birth has access to genius," how would you show up in your world today? Where does your genius live?

And if you knew that everyone by virtue of his birth has access to loving, how would you show up in your world today? Where does your loving live?

31 · HOT SUMMER NIGHTS IN VIRGINIA

Both authors Byron Katie and Steven Dahl wrote, "True forgiveness is realizing there's nothing to forgive."

What does that statement mean to you? Can you see the truth of it clearly, like when the sun is shining, or is the meaning more obscure, like at night when there is no moon?

I chased fireflies as a child, what did you chase? How did you think the world worked? Can you see that you were doing the best you could? Can you see that everyone, based on how they think the world works, is doing the best they can?

Henry Wadsworth Longfellow said, "If we could read the secret history of our enemies, we should find in each man's life sorrow and suffering enough to disarm all hostility."

How could you apply this statement in your relationships with others? How could you apply it in your relationship with yourself?

Do you think that it's accurate that your own purity, stillness, sweetness and love never leave you, you simply lose sight of them? Are you willing to consider it might be accurate and identify those qualities in yourself? In others?

In what ways are you or have you been cultivating purity and stillness or sweetness and love? What thoughts would support you in further cultivation of these qualities that you could think over and over again, like Thoreau said?

What have purity and stillness/sweetness and love taught you? Is there anything or anyone you're willing to accept exactly as they are without forcing them to be anything or anyone else?

32 · The Code that Unlocks the Safe

Theologian and philosopher St. Augustine said 21 centuries ago, "Free curiosity is of more value than harsh discipline."

What evidence in your life do you have that "free curiosity is of more value than harsh discipline"? What does "free curiosity" mean to you?

As you review the code contained within each chapter, what part of the code resonate most within you? In what ways can you support yourself daily in using this code that unlocks the safe of your heart?

What codes or statements of intention return you to the truth of who you are daily, supporting you in releasing the extraordinary coded within?

Are there other pieces of the code or combinations of codes that you found written within the pages of this book? If so, what?

What creative ways have you found to practice unlocking the safe of your heart? What supports you in experiencing a return to the sanctuary of your loving heart again and again, being restored to the truth of who you are over and over?

As you reflect on ways of being gentle, loving and patient with yourself and others, as you allow these things to get drawn out from within, slowly over time, what possibilities come forward?

33 · INSIDE THE SANCTUARY OF OUR UNLOCKED HEARTS

If you knew there was no hurry and there was nothing to worry about either, how would you show up in your world today?

If living well means loving well, in what ways could you show up more in your loving? In what ways could you live more fully in the awareness that you are a divine loving being having a human experience?

Mary Oliver's poem "Wild Geese" is such a beautiful illustration of the benevolent nature of the universe. In your life, list three examples of how the world "offers itself to your imagination, announcing your place in the family of things."

When you go out of balance, what are some ways you've discovered to bring yourself back into balance? What are some ways that you align with love or the great heart of the universe?

If you were to choose a quality that best describes you from the list of extraordinary treasures coded within your heart on pages 228-229, which quality would you choose?

Which qualities, if consciously cultivated, might radically transform your inner world and revolutionize your outer world, too?

CONCLUSION:
Consciousness Is Its Own Reward

What messages might your dreams be trying to communicate to you?

If you knew that consciousness is its own reward, how might you cultivate your own unconditionally loving consciousness, calling forward the beauty of your own being?

Vietnamese Zen Buddhist monk Thich Nhat Hanh said, "The miracle is not to walk on water. The miracle is to walk on the green earth, dwelling deeply in the present moment and feeling truly alive." In what ways could you align with and participate in the miracle today?

When I imagined residing in an unconditionally loving consciousness, the metaphor of walking through all those industrial-looking doors occurred to me. When you imagine residing in an unconditionally loving consciousness, what metaphors occur to you?

What would your life look like if you saw it through the lens of the spiritual consciousness, if you looked at your life and yourself through the soft eyes of love?

INDEX

"I will go before your face.

I will be on your right hand and on your left,

my Spirit shall be in your hearts,

and mine angels round about you,

to bear you up."

Doctrine and Covenants 84:88

ACKNOWLEDGEMENTS

There's a sign hanging over the doorway that leads to my daughters' rooms that reads, "I believe in angels." It's true. I really do believe in angels. I believe in angels because the writing of this book would not have been possible without the following angels who have surrounded, protected and enfolded me with their love, abundantly and generously blessing my life.

Drs. Ron and Mary Hulnick, Co-Directors and Founding Faculty at the University of Santa Monica: Without the impeccable programs in Spiritual Psychology and Consciousness, Health and Healing that you've co-created over the past 30 years, this book would not nor could not have been written. I thank you both for modeling for me what it means to reside in an unconditionally loving consciousness. Heartfelt thanks as well for drawing the divine being out from within me and for teaching me to use everything for my learning, growth and upliftment. Your sweetness, strength of heart and devotion to serving Spirit changed my life, making it better, way better and a whole lot more gorgeous, too.

USM Spiritual Psychology Class of 2011; Consciousness, Health and Healing Class of 2012; and Soul-Centered Professional Coaching Class of 2013; all my USM classmates: Spending those years with you "out beyond ideas of right-doing and wrong-doing," in Rumi's field, healed me, restoring me to the essence of who I truly am. You are my SweeTarts, my Peeps, my Xtremely Bubblicious LifeSavers and Sugar Daddies on the Rocky Road of life. Each one of you is a Gold Nugget, a Hot Tamale, an Atomic Fireball, a divine being worth more than 100 Grand.

Steve Chandler, my astonishing coach: Thank you for sharing your many years of wit and wisdom with me and for boldly being my Secretariat, encouraging me to let the big horse run. Running in your slipstream has been a great blessing and privilege. Your genius, power and magic inspire me to live a fully creative life.

Stellasue Lee, Ph.D., my writing coach: The loveliness of your laughter and your words of encouragement will play like music in my ears forever. Thank you for calling me a writer and for reminding me that writing was written into my contract for this life.

Chris Molé, my book designer: What a treasure you are. Thank you for your patience with me as we brought this book into form. I appreciate the loving and gentle way you worked with me as we designed the interior and exterior of this book, the beauty of which far exceeds my expectations.

Kathy Eimers, my editor: This is a better book because of you. Thank you for your excellent editing and for your deliciously thorough and satisfying explanations of why grammar works the way it does. You shine very bright.

Jessica Cash, my proofreader and sister-in-law: In the midst of a very busy time in your life, I thank you for proofreading my book. The blessing of you and the vintage romantic qualities that you embody goes on and on.

Carrie Henkel-Brito: Your generous and loving offer to design the cover of this book inspired me right into writing it. Thank you for getting things started then handing your beautiful work off to me when Baby Brito arrived.

Connie Smith, my friend and beta-reader: Many years ago, you were the safe place I went, close to home, when nowhere felt safe. Your ceaseless support and fearless friendship are gifts of the highest order. Thank you for your enthusiasm for this book, your confidence in me and your endless love.

Monica Heslington, my American friend who I met in Paris: Your gentle and steady presence has been a blessing over many years now. Thank you for being the most overqualified babysitter to ever live and for helping me with my girls when they were young. Thank you, too, for your willingness to read this book quickly, checking for errors. You're a living blessing.

Kimberly Ablard McGowan, my best buddy pal forever: You said to me many years ago that maturity is the ability to endure uncertainty. As I endured so much uncertainty, you modeled maturity for me. My deep appreciation and love for you are best expressed in the words of Elton John and Kee Kee Dee. Their words were the very ones we sang over and over to each other 40 years ago, "Right from the start, I gave you my heart." Thank you for holding my heart with such grace, such care, such love.

McCall, Madison and Hadley, my daughters: You remind me every day what it means to be genuinely good and extraordinarily brave. What an honor it is to be your mom. I thank you with my whole heart for loving me through it all. I love you, too, no matter what, forever.

Eric Savage, my sweetheart: Your quiet strength and ongoing love bring me to tears. Thank you for taking care of everything while I wrote—me, my girls, my dog, my bunny, my house, car, computer, phone, plane tickets, groceries, dinner, everything. Thank you for taking such good care of everything. You are "the bird with a leaf in his mouth after the flood when the colors came out" that U2 told me would come.

My Mom and Dad, three sisters, one brother, three brothers -in-law, one sister-in-law, eight nephews, nine nieces and again my three daughters, my family: My gratitude for you I save for last since you are the steady foundation that makes everything else possible. In the words of Victor Hugo's Jean Val Jean, "My soul belongs to God, I know. I made that bargain long ago. He gave me hope when hope was gone. He gave me strength to journey on." You are the angels who have surrounded me my whole life, the angels doing God's work here on Earth. You gave me hope when hope was gone. You gave me strength to journey on. My gratitude and love goes on and on and on, forever and ever.

LORI CASH RICHARDS, M.A. is a graduate of the University of Santa Monica where she earned her master's degree in Spiritual Psychology with an emphasis in Consciousness, Health and Healing. She is also a graduate of USM's Soul-Centered Professional Coaching program. Her work as a writer, life coach, workshop facilitator and speaker centers on serving global transformation in consciousness by focusing on transformation of consciousness in the individual. She lives in Palos Verdes, California, with her three daughters.

For information about coaching, workshops and talks, please contact:

Lori Cash Richards
The Winford Group
955 Deep Valley Drive #2523
Palos Verdes, CA 90274
www.loricashrichards.com

NOTES

NOTES

NOTES

NOTES

NOTES

FACING WEST:

The Metaphysics
of Indian-Hating and
Empire-Building